Prefaces and Forewords of Dr. Ambedkar

Compiled by

RATNESH KATULKAR

DEDICATION

This book is dedicated to Vasant Moon, LR Balley, and Bhagwan Das - three legendary Ambedkarite writers who protected, preserved, and propagated the writings of Dr. Babasaheb Ambedkar to enlighten the masses.

Contents

Preface

Writing a preface for a book that compiles Dr Ambedkar's prefaces and forewords is truly a wonderful experience. One may question the need for such a book, as these writings are already available in the public domain. The answer is of course, they are but they are scattered across the 17 volumes of Dr Babasaheb Ambedkar Writings and Speeches (BAWS), making it difficult for a lay reader to access them all in one place.

The idea of compiling this book came to me one evening while finishing up some work in my office. I took a break and picked up a volume of Dr Ambedkar's writings that was on my desk. I began reading its preface and was immediately drawn in. I had read this book before, but this time, my focus was solely on the preface. Of course, this was not the first instance where I had read Dr Ambedkar's prefaces without reading the entire book. I remembered reading the preface of his famous book, 'The Buddha and His Dhamma.' that I read long years after reading the book. The reason was that when this book was published, this preface was not included in it. Years later this was published in Vol. 17 part two of Dr Babasaheb Writings & Speeches. I thought about all the people who may have missed out on this important preface and realized the necessity of compiling a book with an extensive collection of Dr Ambedkar's prefaces so that all these prefaces could be availed easily in one place. This led me to think of the necessity of creating a book with an extensive collection of his prefaces.

I discussed this plan with my friend Dhamma Darshan Nigam, a keen student of Dalit studies. He became excited with the idea and stressed the importance of making this book as soon as possible. He provided me with a copy of Bhagwan Das's book 'Unpublished Preface of Dr Ambedkar', which contained prefaces that had not been published before.

Many of these prefaces are now available in Vol. 17 part 2 and in some other volumes of writings and speeches of Dr Babasaheb Ambedkar.

The present book is a collection of all the prefaces and Forewords which have become available to me through various sources. Of course, the primary source is Dr Babasaheb Ambedkar Writings and speeches. However, I have also explored other sources to collect the data. One of the forewords 'The Indian Political Riddle' is taken from Bhagwan Das's collection 'Rare Preface of Dr Ambedkar' and the original preface of 'The Buddha and His Dhamma' is from the Colombia University website.

Dr Ambedkar's prefaces are not just formalities of introducing his books, but each one contains his sharp ability to succinctly narrate a problem. Take, for instance, the preface of 'The Untouchables' and 'Who Were the Shudras.' They are so well-written that the essence of his entire thesis is captured in just a few pages. The younger generation, who are always short on time, can get a glimpse of the books by reading these prefaces for just a few minutes.

Compiling this book was not a difficult task, but it did become an added responsibility in my busy schedule. I am grateful to my partner Sevanti and my daughter Roshi, who supported and motivated me throughout the process. Finally I am grateful to Amazon kdp for providing me opportunity to publish this work.

I hope that readers find this book useful and gain a greater appreciation for Dr Ambedkar's literary legacy.

Ratnesh Katulkar

PART 1 AUTOBIOGRAPHY

Dalit writers have found a powerful voice through their autobiographies, which have gained global recognition and been translated into various languages. These personal accounts offer a unique glimpse into the challenges and hardships faced due to their caste, financial obstacles, and other material issues which are absent in the lives of a mainstream individuals. This makes these autobiographies a compelling and insightful read for all.

It's unclear who among Dalits the first to write his biography was. However, it's worth noting that Dr Ambedkar, who is a source of inspiration for many Dalit authors, had also intended to write his autobiography. Sadly, due to his busy schedule, he was unable to find the time to complete it, and the project remains unfinished. In the book "Waiting for Visa" which is available in BAWS Vol.5, Dr. Ambedkar shares his life story and experiences with the hope of raising awareness about the issues of caste and untouchability to foreign readers. His autobiography sheds light on the struggles that he and millions of others faced due to the discriminatory caste system in India. Through his writing, Dr. Ambedkar aims to inspire change and bring an end to this oppressive system.

It is interesting to share that the glimpses of his life struggle were also shared by him to his Indian followers through his speeches. One can remember one specific instance when he was at Kalyan Railway Station, where a meeting was organized by railway workers in support of his conversion movement on 17th May 1936. During this meeting, he narrated some of his life events, which were truly inspiring. His mental struggle and dilemma in his early life also appeared in his preface of 'The Buddha and His Dhamma.' These events truly showcase his resilience and determination towards achieving his goals.

The title of the autobiography itself sheds light on the struggles faced by the author and his community. It's a powerful reminder of the importance of equality and fairness in our society.

Waiting for a Visa

Preface[i]

Foreigners of course know of the existence of untouchability. But not being next door to it, so to say, they are unable to realize how oppressive it is in its actuality. It is difficult for them to understand how it is possible for a few untouchables to live on the edge of a village consisting of a large number of Hindus, go through the village daily to free it from the most disagreeable of its filth and to carry the errands of all the sundry, collect food at the doors of the Hindus, buy spices and oil at the shops of the Hindu Bania from a distance, regard the village in every way as their home, and yet never touch nor be touched by any one belonging to the village. The problem is how best to give an idea of the way the untouchables are treated by the caste Hindus.

A general description or a record of cases of the treatment accorded to them are the two methods by which this purpose could be achieved. I have felt that the latter would be more effective than the former. In choosing these illustrations I have drawn partly upon my experience and partly upon the experience of others. I begin with events that have happened to me in my own life.

***

PART 2 BUDDHISM

Buddhism is one of the favourite topics of Dr Ambedkar. The Buddha and His Dhamma is his famous book. However, what may be less known is that he wrote two different versions of this book. The first version, titled 'The Buddha and His Gospel' had limited circulation and was written for the intellectual leaders of the Buddhist world. Regrettably, Dr. Ambedkar did not receive much feedback on this version, except for one suggestion to use the word Dhamma instead of Gospel. Dr. Ambedkar accepted this advice and titled his second version 'The Buddha and His Dhamma.' Sadly the first version of the book is not available to us. However, a Xeroxed version of this is in the possession of a prominent Ambedkarite scholar Vijay Survade. But, he is not sure whether this is the original copy of the first version or a one of a draft of the second version.

Of course, Dr. Ambedkar had written two different prefaces for these two books and spent a considerable amount of time writing 'The Buddha and His Dhamma.' However, due to his sudden demise, the second version did not appear as per his plan. The People's Education Society and Siddhartha Publication took responsibility for publishing the available manuscript of 'The Buddha and His Dhamma', but it lacked professional copyediting skills. Moreover, the reason best known to them they used the old preface written for 'The Buddha and His Gospel' instead of the original preface written for this book. Thanks to Bhagwan Das, Eleanor Zelliot and Dr Savita Ambedkar this important preface is preserved and made available to us. In this section, both these prefaces are presented for your convenience.

Additionally, it is worth mentioning that apart from his writings, Dr. Ambedkar also took pain in spreading the right teaching of what is now called Navayana Buddhism to people. In this attempt, he found a rare book by PL Narasu 'Essence of Buddhism.' He was so impressed with this book that he took personal responsibility for republishing this book and wrote a foreword, which is informative and enlightening.

The Buddha and His Dhamma

Preface[ii]

A question is always asked to me: how I happened to take such a high degree of education. Another question is being asked: why I am inclined towards Buddhism. These questions are asked because I was born in a community known in India as the "Untouchables." This preface is not the place for answering the first question. But this preface may be the place for answering the second question.

The direct answer to this question is that I regard the Buddha's Dhamma to be the best. No religion can be compared to it. If a modern man who knows science must have a religion, the only religion he can have is the Religion of the Buddha. This conviction has grown in me after thirty-five years of close study of all religions.

How I was led to study Buddhism is another story. It may be interesting for the reader to know. This is how it happened.

My father was a military officer, but at the same time a very religious person. He brought me up under a strict discipline. From my early age I found certain contradictions in my father's religious way of life. He was a Kabirpanthi, though his father was Ramanandi. As such, he did not believe in Murti Puja (Idol Worship), and yet he performed Ganapati Puja--of course for our sake, but I did not like it. He read the books of his Panth. At the same time, he compelled me and my elder brother to read every day before going to bed a portion of the Mahabharata and Ramayana to my sisters and other persons who assembled at my father's house to hear the Katha. This went on for a long number of years.

The year I passed the English Fourth Standard Examination, my community people wanted to celebrate the occasion by holding a public meeting to congratulate me. Compared to the state of education in other communities, this was hardly an occasion for celebration. But it was felt by the organisers that I was the first boy in my community to reach this stage; they thought that I had reached a great height. They went to my father to ask for his permission. My father flatly refused, saying that such a thing would inflate the boy's head; after all, he has only passed an examination and done nothing more. Those who wanted to celebrate the event were greatly disappointed. They, however, did not give way. They went to Dada Keluskar, a personal friend of my father, and asked him to intervene. He agreed. After a little argumentation, my father yielded, and the meeting was held. Dada Keluskar presided. He was a literary person of his time. At the end of his address he gave me as a gift a copy of his book on the life of the Buddha, which he had written for the Baroda Sayajirao Oriental Series. I read the book with great interest, and was greatly impressed and moved by it.

I began to ask why my father did not introduce us to the Buddhist literature. After this, I was determined to ask my father this question. One day I did. I asked my father why he insisted upon our reading the Mahabharata and Ramayana, which recounted the greatness of the Brahmins and the Kshatriyas and repeated the stories of the degradation of the Shudras and the Untouchables. My father did not like the question. He merely said, "You must not ask such silly questions. You are only boys; you must do as you are told." My father was a Roman Patriarch, and exercised most extensive Patria Pretestas over his children. I alone could take a little liberty with him, and that was because my mother had died in my childhood, leaving me to the care of my auntie.

So after some time, I asked again the same question. This time my father had evidently prepared himself for a reply. He said, "The reason why I ask you to read the Mahabharata and Ramayana is this: we belong to the Untouchables, and you are likely to develop an inferiority complex, which is natural. The value of the Mahabharata and Ramayana lies in removing this inferiority complex. See Drona and Karna--they were small men, but to what heights they rose! Look at Valmiki--he was a Koli, but he became the author of the Ramayana. It is for removing this inferiority complex that I ask you to read the Mahabharata and Ramayana."

I could see that there was some force in my father's argument. But I was not satisfied. I told my father that I did not like any of the figures in the Mahabharata. I said, "I do not like Bhishma and Drona, nor Krishna. Bhishma and Drona were hypocrites. They said one thing and did quite the opposite. Krishna believed in fraud. His life is nothing but a series of frauds. Equal dislike I have for Rama. Examine his conduct in the Shurpanakha episode and in the Bali-Sugriva episode, and his beastly behaviour towards Sita." My father was silent, and made no reply. He knew that there was a revolt.

This is how I turned to the Buddha, with the help of the book given to me by Dada Keluskar. It was not with an empty mind that I went to the Buddha at that early age. I had a background, and in reading the Buddhist Lore I could always compare and contrast. This is the origin of my interest in the Buddha and His Dhamma.

The urge to write this book has a different origin. In 1951 the Editor of the Mahabodhi Society's Journal of Calcutta asked me to write an article for the Vaishak Number. In that article I argued that the Buddha's Religion was the only religion which a society awakened by science could accept, and without which it would perish. I also pointed out that for the modern world Buddhism was the only religion which it must have to save itself. That Buddhism makes a slow advance is due to the fact that its literature is so vast that no one can read the whole of it. That it has no such thing as a bible, as the Christians have, is its greatest handicap. On the publication of this article, I received many calls, written and oral, to write such a book. It is in response to these calls that I have undertaken the task.

To disarm all criticism I would like to make it clear that I claim no originality for the book. It is a compilation and assembly plant. The material has been gathered from various books. I would particularly like to mention Ashvaghosha's Buddhacharita, whose poetry no one can excel. In the narrative of certain events I have even borrowed his language.

The only originality that I can claim is the order of presentation of the topics, in which I have tried to introduce simplicity and clarity. There are certain matters which give headaches to the student of Buddhism. I have dealt with them in the Introduction.

It remains for me to express my gratitude to those who have been helpful to me. I am very grateful to Mr. Nanak Chand Rattu of Village Sakrulli and Mr. Parkash Chand of Village Nangal Khurd in the district of Hoshiarpur (Punjab) for the burden they have taken upon themselves to type out the manuscript. They have done it several times. Shri Nanak Chand Rattu took special pains and put in very hard labour in accomplishing this great task. He did the whole work of typing etc. very willingly and without caring for his health and or any sort of remuneration. Both Mr. Nanak Chand Rattu and Mr. Parkash Chand did their job as a token of their greatest love and affection towards me. Their labours can hardly be repaid. I am very much grateful to them.

When I took up the task of composing the book I was ill, and
I am still ill. During these five years there were many ups and
downs in my health. At some stages my condition had
become so critical that doctors talked of me as a dying flame.
The successful rekindling of this dying flame is due to the
medical skill of my wife and Dr. Malvankar. They alone have
helped me to complete the work. I am also thankful to Mr.
M. B. Chitnis, who took a special interest in correcting the
proof and to go in going through the whole book.

I may mention that this is one of the three books which will
form a set for the proper understanding of Buddhism. The
other books are: (i) Buddha and Karl Marx; and
(ii) Revolution and Counter-Revolution in Ancient India.
They are written out in parts. I hope to publish them soon.

B. R. Ambedkar
26 Alipur Road, Delhi
6-4-56

The Buddha and His Gospel

Preface[iii]

Indications of a growth in the volume of interest in Buddhism are noticeable in some sections of the Indian people. Along with it there is naturally a growing demand for a clear and consistent statement of the life and teachings of the Buddha.

Anyone who is not a Buddhist finds it extremely difficult to present the life and teachings of the Buddha in a manner which would make it a consistent whole. Depending on the Nikayas, not only the presentation of a consistent story of the life of the Buddha becomes a difficult thing and the presentation of some parts of his teachings becomes much more so. Indeed it would not be an exaggeration to say that of all the founders of religions in the world, the presentation of the life and teachings of the founder of Buddhism presents a problem which is quite puzzling if not baffling. Is it not necessary that these problems should be solved, and the path for the understanding of Buddhism be made clear? Is it not time that those who are Buddhists should take up these problems, at least for general discussion, and throw what light they can on these problems?

With a view to raise a discussion on these problems, I propose to set them out here. The first problem relates to the main event in the life of the Buddha, namely, Parivraja. Why did the Buddha take Parivraja? The traditional answer is that he took Parivraja because he saw a dead person, a sick person and an old person. This answer is absurd on the face of it. The Buddha took Parivraja at the age of 29. If he took Parivraja as a result of these three sights, how is it he did not see these three sights earlier? These are common events occurring by hundreds, and the Buddha could not have failed to come across them earlier. It is impossible to accept the traditional explanation that this was the first time he saw them. The explanation is not plausible and does not appeal to reason. But if this is not the answer to the question, what is the real answer?

The second problem is created by the four Aryan Truths. Do they form part of the original teachings of the Buddha? This formula cuts at the root of Buddhism. If life is sorrow, death is sorrow, and rebirth is sorrow, then there is an end of everything. Neither religion nor philosophy can help a man to achieve happiness in the world. If there is no escape from sorrow, then what can religion do, what can Buddha do, to relieve man from such sorrow which is ever there in birth itself? The four Aryan Truths are a great stumbling block in the way of non-Buddhists accepting the gospel of Buddhism. For the four Aryan Truths deny hope to man. The four Aryan Truths make the gospel of the Buddha a gospel of pessimism. Do they form part of the original gospel, or are they a later accretion by the monks?

The third problem relates to the doctrines of soul, of karma and rebirth. The Buddha denied the existence of the soul. But he is also said to have affirmed the doctrine of karma and rebirth. At once a question arises. If there is no soul, how can there be karma? If there is no soul, how can there be rebirth? These are baffling questions. In what sense did the Buddha use the words karma and rebirth? Did he use them in a different sense than the sense in which they were used by the Brahmins of his day? If so, in what sense? Did he use them in the same sense in which the Brahmins used them? If so, is there not a terrible contradiction between the denial of the soul and the affirmation of karma and rebirth? This contradiction needs to be resolved.

The fourth problem relates to the Bhikkhu. What was the object of the Buddha in creating the Bhikkhu? Was the object to create a perfect man? Or was his object to create a social servant devoting his life to service of the people and being their friend, guide and philosopher? This is a very real question. On it depends the future of Buddhism. If the Bhikkhu is only a perfect man he is of no use to the propagation of Buddhism, because though a perfect man he is a selfish man. If, on the other hand, he is a social servant, he may prove to be the hope of Buddhism. This question must be decided not so much in the interest of doctrinal consistency but in the interest of the future of Buddhism.

If I may say so, the pages of the journal of the Mahabodhi Society make, to me at any rate, dull reading. This is not because the material presented is not interesting and instructive. The dullness is due to the fact that it seems to fall upon a passive set of readers. After reading an article, one likes to know what the reader of the journal has to say about it. But the reader never gives out his reaction. This silence on the part of the reader is a great discouragement to the writer. I hope my questions will excite the readers to come and make their contribution to their solution.

The Essence of Buddhism

Foreword[iv]

The author of this book was Prof. P. Lakshmi Narasu. While I have great pleasure in introducing this book to the public I confess that I had not met the author and known very little about his personal life. I have tried to obtain whatever details that could be gathered about his personal life and literary work. For this purpose, I have found Dr, Pattabhi Sitaramayya to be the source. He knew Prof. Narasu personally and was a friend of his. I give below the main facts in the life of Prof. Narasu as given to me by Dr. Pattabhi. Prof. P. Lakshmi Narasu, B.A., was a prodigy of the last century. He was a graduate in Physics from the Madras Christian College. From being a tutor and demonstrator, he rose to the position of an Assistant Professor by 1897 and was given full charge of Physics and Chemistry for the B. A. classes in 1898-99, during the absence of Prof. Moffatt, the permanent Professor of Physics on leave. Prof. Moffatt was a raw youth who was appointed to the professorship over the head of Prof. Narasu who had already won his distinction in Physics in the sphere of wireless telegraphy – which in the nineties of the last century as yet in its infant stage of progress. During the years 1898 and 1899 Prof. Narasu, as he used to be called in those days, was already an Examiner in Physics and Chemistry — both for B. A. and M. A. Examinations.

Prof. Narasu was particularly strong in Dynamics. Once when an alteration arose over the correctness of a question in Dynamics, Prof. Wilson, a hot-headed Englishman who was Professor of Chemistry in the Presidency College, Madras and Chairman of the Board of Examiners in Physics and Chemistry, questioned the correctness of the view expressed by Prof. Narasu regarding some problem in Dynamics. Prof. Narasu took up the challenge at once. 'Do you want to teach me, Mr. Narasu' asked the arrogant Wilson to which in reply Prof. Narasu retorted -after working out the problem — 'I am glad I am teaching Prof. Wilson something in Dynamics.' The incident is of interest to us fifty years after its occurrence, because it shows that Prof. Narasu was an Iconoclast.

Prof. Narasu was a Social Reformer. He fought caste to the best of his ability and raised the standard of Revolt against its tyranny in Hinduism, so early as in the nineties of the 18th century. He was a great admirer of Buddhism and gave courses of lectures on the subject week in and week out. He was highly popular with his students over whom he exercised a magical personal influence so as to broaden their outlook and widen their visions. His sense of self-respect, both personal and national was of a high order and he did not stand the arrogance and sense of self superiority of his European colleagues to whom he was always ready to give their due in the domain of scholarship but at whose hands he would not take insults lying down. Prof. Narasu's eminence as an Educationist did not take long to obtain general and widespread recognition and era long he was promoted to the Principalship of the Pachiappa's College.

Prof. Narasu was a highly public-spirited citizen and took active part in the organization of a body known as the ' National Fund and Industrial Association' under whose auspices, petty donations were being collected with which aid was rendered to students who desired to go abroad for advanced technical education. Japan was the country which attracted the young man of the day and it was their ambition to learn the technique of various small industries and manufactures - notably - soap making, enamelling and paints manufacture and so on. But the Professor's one sin was social reform and in Buddhism he found his solace. He was one of the earliest to discern the evils of the caste system, early marriages and prohibition of widow marriage and it was then considered in Reform Circles a matter for gratification that one of his brothers was a practical Social Reformer, having married a widow. That was the era when Christian Missionaries were not only countenancing the social reform movement but viewed it with high favour as marking a half-way house between orthodox Hinduism and conversion to Christianity. It did not take long for them to change their views and look upon such progressive movements as constituting a real hindrance to proselytization.

Prof. Narasu was the stalwart of the 19th century who had fought European arrogance with patriotic fervour, orthodox Hinduism with iconoclastic zeal, heterodox Brahmins with nationalistic vision and aggressive Christianity with a rationalistic outlook - all under the inspiring banner of his unflagging faith in the teachings of the Great Buddha. In recent times many people from different parts of India have been asking me to recommend a good book on Buddhism. In responding to their wishes, I felt no hesitation in suggesting Prof. Narasu's book. For, I think that it is the best book on Buddhism that has appeared so far. Unfortunately, the book has been out of print for a long time. I, therefore, decided to reprint it so that the desire of those who have an interest in the teachings of Buddhism may have in their hand a text which is complete in its treatment and lucid in its exposition.

I must thank the representatives of the old firm of Varadachari and Co., Madras, who held the copy right of the original publication for permission to reprint the book. In writing this foreword to this reprint, it was my intention to deal with some of the Criticisms which have been levelled against the teachings of Buddha by his adversaries—past and present. I have given up that intention for two reasons. In the first place, my health will not permit me to engage myself in this task.

Secondly, I am myself working on a Life of Buddha and I think that I could deal with this matter better in my own work wherein I could do more justice to it than in a foreword to another man's work. I have taken this decision more especially because I am sure that the reader of Prof. Narasu's book will not suffer in any way as a result of my decision.

B. R. Ambedkar
"RAJ GRAHA," HINDU COLONY, DADAR,
BOMBAY 14.
10th March 1948

PART 3 HINDUISM

Dr Ambedkar devoted a significant part of his life to studying Hinduism and concluded that this religion is at the root of many of India's socio-economic and political problems. He made a courageous decision to renounce Hinduism, declaring in his Yeola statement that he would not die as a Hindu. His book 'Riddles in Hinduism' sparked controversy and was even considered for a ban in India. Nevertheless, Ambedkarites fought for the book's availability, and it is now easily accessible to us.

Riddles in Hinduism

Introduction[v]

This book is an exposition of the beliefs propounded by what might be called Brahmanic theology. It is intended for the common mass of Hindus who need to be awakened to know in what quagmire the Brahmins have placed them and to lead them on to the road of rational thinking.

The Brahmins have propagated the view that the Hindu civilization is Sanatan, that is, unchanging. This view has been reinforced by a good many of the European Scholars who have said that the Hindu civilization is static. In this book I have attempted to show that this view is not in accord with facts and that Hindu Society has changed from time to time and that often times the change is of the most radical kind. In this connection, compare the Riddles from Himsa to Ahimsa and from Ahimsa back to Himsa. I want to make the mass of people to realize that Hindu religion is not Sanatan.

The second purpose of this book is to draw attention of the Hindu masses to the devices of the Brahmins and to make them think for themselves how they have been deceived and misguided by the Brahmins.

It will be noticed how the Brahmins have changed and chopped. There was a time when they worshipped the Vedic Gods. Then came a time when they abandoned their Vedic Gods and started worshipping non-Vedic Gods. One may well ask them—where is Indra, where is Varuna, where is Brahma, where is Mitra — the Gods mentioned in the Vedas? They have all disappeared. And why, because the worship of Indra, Varuna and Brahma ceased to be profitable. Not only did the Brahmins abandon their Vedic Gods but there are cases where they have become the worshippers of Muslim

Pirs. In this connection one glaring case may be referred to. In Kalyan near Bombay there is a famous Darga of Pir called Bawa Malangsha on the top of a hill. It is a very famous Darga. Every year aUrs(pilgrimage) is held and offerings are made. The person who officiates at the Darga as a priest is a Brahmin, sitting near it, wearing the clothes of Muslims and receiving monies offered at the Darga. This he did for the sake of money. Religion or no religion what the Brahmin wants is Dakshina. Indeed the Brahmins have made religion a matter of trade and commerce.

Compare with this faithlessness of the Brahmins the fidelity of the Jews to their Gods even when their conqueror Nebuchadnezzar forced the Jews to abandon their religion and adopt his (religion).[vi]

Nebuchadnezzar, the king, made an image of gold, whose height was three score cubits, and the breadth thereof six cubits; he set it up in the plain of Dura, in the province of Babylon. Nebuchadnezzar, the king, ordered the princes, the governors, the captains, the judges, the treasurers, the counsellors, the sheriffs, and all the rulers of the provinces to come to the dedication of the image which Nebuchadnezzar, the king had set up.

Then the princes, the governors, the captains, the judges, the treasurers, the counsellors, the sheriffs, and all the rulers of the provinces, were gathered together unto the dedication of the image that Nebuchadnezzar the king had set up; and they stood before the image that Nebuchadnezzar had set up.

Then an herald cried aloud, "To you, it is commanded, O people, nations, and languages, That at what time ye hear the sound of the cornet, flute, harp, sack-but, psaltery, dulcimer and all kinds of musick, ye fall down and worship the golden image that Nebuchadnezzar the king hath set up: And who so falleth not down and worshippeth shall the same hour be cast into the midst of burning fiery furnace."

Therefore at that time, when all the people heared the sound of the cornet, flute, harp, sack-but, psaltery, dulcimer, and all kinds of musick, all the people, the nations, and the languages fell down and worshipped the golden image that Nebuchadnezzar the king had set up.

Wherefore at that time certain Chaldeans came near, and accused the Jews.

They spake and said to the king Nebuchadnezzar, "O King, live forever. Thou, O king, hast made a decree, that every man that shall hear the sound of the cornet, flute, harp, sack-but, psaltery, dulcimer, and all kinds of musick shall fall down and worship the golden image; And who so falleth not down and worshippeth that he should be cast into the midst of a burning fiery furnace; There are certain Jews whom thou hast set over the affairs of the province of Babylon; Shadrach, Meshach, and Abed-nego; these men, O king, have not regarded thee; they serve not thy gods, nor worship the golden image which thou hast set up."

Then Nebuchadnezzar in his rage and fury commanded to bring Shadrach, Meshach, and Abed-nego. Then they brought these men before king. Nebuchadnezzar spake and said unto them, "Is it true, O Shadrach, Meshach and Abed-nego, do not ye serve my gods, nor worship the golden image which I have set up? Now if ye'be ready that at what time ye hear the sound of the cornet, flute, harp, sack-but, psaltery, and dulcimer, and all kinds of musick, ye fall down and worship the image which I have made; well! but if ye worship not, ye shall be cast the same hour into the midst of a burning fiery furnace; and who is that God that shall deliver you out of my hands?" Shadrach, Meshach, and Abed-nego, answered and said to the king, "O Nebuchadnezzar, we are not careful to answer thee in this matter. If it be so, our God whom we serve is able to deliver us from the burning fiery furnace and he will deliver us out of thine hand, O King. But if not, be it known unto thee, O King, that we will not serve thy Gods, nor worship the golden image which thou hast set up." Then was Nebuchadnezzar full of fury, and the form of his visage was changed against Shadrach, Meshach, and Abed-nego; therefore he spake, and commanded that they should heat the furnace one seven times more than it was wont to be heated. And he commanded the most mighty men that were in his army to bind Shadrach, Meshach, and Abed-nego, and to cast them into the burning fiery furnace. Then these men were bound in their coats, their hosen and their hats, and their other garments, and were cast into the midst of the burning fiery furnace. Therefore because the king's commandment was urgent, and the furnace exceeding hot, the flame of the fire slew those men that took up Shadrach, Meshach, and Abed-nego. And these three men, Shadrach, Meshach, and Abed-nego, fell down bound into the midst of the burning fiery furnace."

Can the Brahmins of India show such stead-fast faith and attachment for their Gods and to their religious faith?

Buckle in his history of civilization says: "It is evident that until doubt began, progress was impossible. For as we have clearly seen, the advance of civilization solely depends on the acquisitions made by the human intellect and on the extent to which those acquisitions are diffused. But men who are perfectly satisfied with their own knowledge will never attempt to increase it. Men who are perfectly convinced of the accuracy of their opinions will never take the pains of examining the basis on which they are built. They look with wonder, and often with horror, on views contrary to those which they inherited from their fathers; and while they are in this state of mind, it is impossible that they should receive any new truth which interferes with their foregone conclusions.

On this account it is, that although the acquisition of fresh knowledge is the necessary precursor of every step in social progress, such acquisition must itself be preceded by a love of inquiry, and therefore by a spirit of doubt; because without doubt there will be no inquiry and without inquiry there will be no knowledge. For knowledge is not an inert and passive principle which comes to us whether we will or not; but it must be sought before it can be won; it is the product of great labour and therefore of great sacrifice. And it is absurd to suppose that men will incur the labour, and make the sacrifice for subjects respecting which they are already perfectly content.

They who do not feel the darkness, will never look for the light. If on any point we have attained to certainty, we make no further inquiry on that point; because inquiry would be useless, or perhaps dangerous. The doubt must intervene, before the investigation can begin. Here, than we have the act of doubting as the originator or, at all events, the necessary antecedent of all progress."

Now the Brahmins have left no room for doubt, for they have propounded a most mischievous dogma which the Brahmins have spread among the masses, is the dogma of the infallibility of the Vedas. If the Hindu intellect has ceased to grow and if the Hindu civilization and culture has become a stagnant and stinking pool, this dogma must be destroyed root and branch if India is to progress. The Vedas are a worthless set of books. There is no reason either to call them sacred or infallible. The Brahmins have invested it with sanctity and infallibility only because by a later interpolation of what is called the Purusha — Sukta, the Vedas have made them the lords of the Earth. Nobody has had the courage to ask why these worthless books which contain nothing but invocation to tribal Gods to destroy the Enemies, loot their property and give it to their followers (have been made sacred and infallible). But the time has come when the Hindu mind must be freed from the hold* which the silly ideas propagated by the Brahmins, have on them. Without this liberation India has no future. I have undertaken this task knowing full well what risk it involves. I am not afraid of the consequences. I shall be happy if I succeed in stirring the masses.

B. R. AMBEDKAR

PART 4 CASTE

Dr Ambedkar's first academic writing was based on the topic of caste. He presented a paper before Anthropology Seminar of Dr AA Goldenweizer, Columbia University on 9th May 1916. He later expanded upon by adding more factual information and explanation. Unfortunately, he was unable to complete this task. This incomplete work can be found in BAWS Vol 3. Since it was an academic paper, there is no preface written for it. However, Dr Ambedkar's other important work on caste was his talk 'Annihilation of Caste.' The organizing committee of the conference found this talk so extreme that they requested Dr Ambedkar to censor it. However, he was confident that none of his words were misleading, and therefore he declined to accept this suggestion. As a consequence, the conference was cancelled. However, he published this talk. It became so popular that he published it twice more. In this section, we present the two prefaces, the preface of the second edition and preface of the third edition.

In addition to this, other writings of Dr Ambedkar are included in this section. He not only studied caste in terms of concept and theory, but he also delved deep to probe its historical roots. His research on Shudras and Untouchables is remarkable in the field of history. The introduction of his essays on Untouchables and Untouchability is also included in this part, and finally, a foreword written by him for author GR Pradhan is presented.

Annihilation of Caste

Preface to the Second Edition[vii]

The speech prepared by me for the Jat-Pat-Todak Mandal of Lahore has had an astonishingly warm reception from the Hindu public for whom it was primarily intended. The English edition of one thousand five hundred was exhausted within two months of its publication. It is translated into Gujarati and Tamil. It is being translated in Marathi, Hindi, Punjabi and Malayalam. The demand for the English text still continues unabated. To satisfy this demand it has become necessary to issue a Second Edition. Considerations of history and effectiveness of appeal have led me to retain the original form of the essay—namely the speech form—although I was asked to recast it in the form of a direct narrative. To this edition I have added two appendices. I have collected in Appendix I the two articles written by Mr. Gandhi by way of review of my speech in the Harijan, and his letter to Mr. Sant Ram, a member of the Jat-Pat-Todak Mandal. In Appendix II, I have printed my views in reply to the articles of Mr. Gandhi collected in Appendix I. Besides Mr. Gandhi many others have adversely criticised my views as expressed in my speech. But I have felt that in taking notice of such adverse comments I should limit myself to Mr. Gandhi. This I have done not because what he has said is so weighty as to deserve a reply but because to many a Hindu he is an oracle, so great that when he opens his lips it is expected that the argument must close and no dog must bark. But the world owes much to rebels who would dare to argue in the face of the pontiff and insist that he is not infallible. I do not care for the credit

which every progressive society must give to its rebels. I shall
be satisfied if I make the Hindus realize that they are the sick
men of India and that their sickness is causing danger to the
health and happiness of other Indians.

35

B. R. AMBEDKAR

Preface to the Third Edition

The Second edition of this Essay appeared in 1937, and was exhausted within a very short period. A new edition has been in demand for a long time. It was my intention to recast the essay so as to incorporate into it another essay of mine called "Castes in India, their Origin and their Mechanism", which appeared in the issue of the Indian Antiquary Journal for May 1917. But as I could not find time, and as there is very little prospect of my being able to do so and as the demand for it from the public is very insistent, I am content to let this be a mere reprint of the Second edition. I am glad to find that this essay has become so popular, and I hope that it will serve the purpose for which it was intended.

B. R. AMBEDKAR

22, Prithwiraj Road, New Delhi
1st December 1944

Who Were the Shudras

In the present stage of the literature on the subject, a book on the Shudras cannot be regarded as a superfluity. Nor can it be said to deal with a trivial problem. The general proposition that the social organization of the Indo-Aryans was based on the theory of Chaturvarnya and that Chaturvarnya means division of society into four classes—Brahmins (priests), Kshatriyas (soldiers),Vaishyas (traders) and Shudras (menials) does not convey any idea of the real nature of the problem of the Shudras nor of its magnitude. Chaturvarnya would have been a very innocent principle if it meant no more than mere division of society into four classes.

Unfortunately, more than this is involved in the theory of Chaturvarnya. Besides dividing society into four orders, the theory goes further and makes the principle of graded inequality the basis for determining the terms of associated life as between the four Varnas. Again, the system of graded inequality is not merely notional. It is legal and penal. Under the system of Chaturvarnya, the Shudra is not only placed at the bottom of the gradation but he is subjected to innumerable ignominies and disabilities so as to prevent him from rising above the condition fixed for him by law. Indeed until the fifth Varna of the Untouchables came into being, the Shudras were in the eyes of the Hindus the lowest of the low. This shows the nature of what might be called the problem of the Shudras. If people have no idea of the magnitude of the problem it is because they have not cared to know what the population of the Shudras is. Unfortunately, the census does not show their population separately. But there is no doubt that excluding the Untouchables the Shudras form about 75 to 80 per cent of the population of Hindus.

A treatise which deals with so vast a population cannot be considered to be dealing with a trivial problem. The book deals with the Shudras in the Indo-Aryan Society. There is a view that an inquiry into these questions is of no present-day moment. It is said by no less a person than Mr. Sherring in his Hindu Tribes and Castes1 that : "Whether the Shudras were Aryans, or aboriginal inhabitants of India, or tribes produced by the union of the one with the other, is of little practical moment. They were at an early period placed in a class by themselves, and received the fourth or last degree of rank, yet at a considerable distance from the three superior castes. Even though it be admitted that at the outset they were not Aryans, still, from their extensive intermarriages with the three Aryan Castes, they have become so far Aryanized that, in some instances as already shown, they have gained more than they have lost, and certain tribes now designated as Shudras are in reality more Brahmins and Kshatriyas than anything else. In short, they have become as much absorbed in other races as the Celtic tribes of England have become absorbed in the Anglo-Saxon race; and their own separate individuality, if they ever had any, has completely vanished." This view is based on two errors.

Firstly, the present-day Shudras are a collection of castes drawn from heterogeneous stocks and are racially different from the original Shudras of the Indo-Aryan society. Secondly, in the case of Shudras the centre of interest is not the Shudras as a people but the legal system of pains and penalties to which they are subjected. The system of pains and penalties was no doubt originally devised by the Brahmins to deal with the Shudras of the Indo-Aryan society, who have ceased to exist as a distinct, separate, identifiable community. But strange as it may seem the Code intended to deal with them has remained in operation and is now applied to all low-class Hindus, who have no lock stock with the original Shudras. How this happened must be a matter of curiosity to all.

My explanation is that the Shudras of the Indo-Aryan Society in course of time became so degraded as a consequence of the severity of the Brahmanical laws that they really came to occupy a very low state in public life. Two consequences followed from this. One consequence was a change in the connotation of the word Shudra. The word Shudra lost its original meaning of being the name of a particular community and became a general name for a low-class people without civilization, without culture, without respect and without position. The second consequence was that the widening of the meaning of the word Shudra brought in its train the widening of the application of the Code. It is in this way that the so-called Shudras of the present-day have become subject to the Code, though they are not Shudras in the original sense of the word. Be that as it may, the fact remains that the Code intended for the original culprits has come to be applied to the innocents. If the Hindu law-givers had enough historical sense to realize that the original Shudras were different from the present-day low-class people, this tragedy—this massacre of the innocents—would have been avoided. The fact, however unfortunate it may be, is that the Code is applied to the present-day Shudras in the same rigorous manner in which it was applied to the original Shudras. How such a Code came into being cannot therefore be regarded as of mere antiquarian interest to the Shudras of today. While it may be admitted that a study of the origin of the Shudras is welcome, some may question my competence to handle the theme. I have already been warned that while I may have a right to speak on Indian politics, religion and religious history of India are not my field and that I must not enter it. I do not know why my critics have thought it necessary to give me this warning. If it is an antidote to any extravagant claim made by me as a thinker or a writer, then it is unnecessary. For, I am ready to admit that I am not competent to speak even on Indian politics. If the warning is for the reason that I cannot claim mastery over the Sanskrit language, 'I admit this deficiency. But I do not see why it should disqualify me altogether from operating in this field. There is very little of literature in the Sanskrit language which is not available in English.

The want of knowledge of Sanskrit need not therefore be a bar to my handling a theme such as the present. For I venture to say that a study of the relevant literature, albeit in English translations, for 15 years ought to be enough to invest even a person endowed with such moderate intelligence like myself, with sufficient degree of competence for the task. As to the exact measure of my competence to speak on the subject, this book will furnish the best testimony. It may well turn out that this attempt of mine is only an illustration of the proverbial fool rushing in where the angels fear to tread. But I take refuge in the belief that even the fool has a duty to perform, namely, to do his bit if the angel has gone to sleep or is unwilling to proclaim the truth.

This is my justification for entering the prohibited field. What is it that is noteworthy about this book? Undoubtedly the conclusions which I have reached as a result of my investigations. Two questions are raised in this book: (1) Who were the Shudras? and (2) How they came to be the fourth Varna of the Indo-Aryan society? My answers to them are summarized below : (1) The Shudras were one of the Aryan communities of the Solar race. (2) There was a time when the Aryan society recognized only three Varnas, namely, Brahmins, Kshatriyas and Vaishyas. (3) The Shudras did not form a separate Varna. They ranked as part of the Kshatriya Varna in the Indo-Aryan society. (4) There was a continuous feud betwen the Shudra kings and the Brahmins in which the Brahmins were subjected to many tyrannies and indignities. (5) As a result of the hatred towards the Shudras generated by their tyrannies and oppressions, the Brahmins refused to perform the Upanayana of the Shudras. (6) Owing to the denial of Upanayana, the Shudras who were Kshatriyas became socially degraded, fell below the rank of the Vaishyas and thus came to form the fourth Varna. I must of course await the verdict of scholars on these conclusions. That these conclusions are not merely original but they are violently opposed to those that are current is of course evident. Whether these conclusions will be accepted or not will depend upon the mentality of a person claiming to have a right to sit in judgement over the issue. Of course, if he is attached to a particular thesis he will reject mine. I would not however bother about his judgement for he would be an adversary from whom nothing can be expected except opposition.

But if a person is an honest critic, howsoever cautious, however conservative he may be, provided that he has an open mind and a readiness to accept facts, I do not despair of converting him to my view. This expectation may fail to materialize, but about one thing I am quite certain. My critics will have to admit that the book is rich in fresh insights and new visions. Apart from scholars, how the Hindu public will react may be an interesting speculation. The Hindus of to-day fall into five definite classes. There is a class of Hindus, who are known as orthodox and who will not admit that there is anything wrong with the Hindu social system. To talk of reforming it is to them rank blasphemy. There is a class of Hindus who are known as Arya Samajists. They believe in the Vedas and only in the Vedas. They differ from the orthodox inasmuch as they discard everything which is not in the Vedas. Their gospel is that of return to the Vedas. There is a class of Hindus who will admit that the Hindu social system is all wrong, but who hold that there is no necessity to attack it. Their argument is that since law does not recognize it, it is a dying, if not a dead system. There is a class of Hindus, who are politically minded. They are indifferent to such questions.

To them Swaraj is more important than social reform. The fifth class of Hindus are those who are rationalists and who regard social reforms as of primary importance, even more important than Swaraj

With the Hindus, who fall into the second category, those who are likely to regard the book as unnecessary, I cannot agree. In a way, they are right when they say that the existing law in British India does not recognize the caste system prevalent in the Hindu society. It is true that, having regard to section 11 of the Civil Procedure Code, it would not be possible for a Hindu to obtain a declaration from a civil court that he belongs to a particular Varna. If courts in British India have to consider the question whether a person belongs to a particular Varna, it is only in cases of marriage, inheritance and adoption, the rules of which vary according to the Varna to which the party belongs. While it is true that the Law in British India does not recognize the four Varnas of the Hindus, one must be careful not to misunderstand what this means. To put it precisely: (1) it does not mean that the observance of the Varna system is a crime; (2) it does not mean that the Varna system has disappeared; (3) it does not mean that the Varna system is not given effect to in cases where the observance of its rules are necessary to acquiring civil rights; (4) it only means that the general legal sanction behind the Varna system has been withdrawn. Now, law is not the only sanction which goes to sustain social institutions. Institutions are sustained by other sanctions also. Of these, religious sanction and social sanction are the most important.

The Varna system has a religious sanction. Because it has a religious sanction, the Varna system has the fullest social sanction from the Hindu society. With no legal prohibition, this religious sanction has been more than enough to keep the Varna system in full bloom. The best evidence to show that the Varna system is alive notwithstanding there is no law to enforce it, is to be found in the fact that the status of the

Shudras and the Untouchables in the Hindu society has remained just what it has been. It cannot therefore be said that a study such as this is unnecessary. As to the politically-minded Hindu, he need not be taken seriously. His line of approach is generally governed by a short-term view more than by long-range considerations. He is willing to follow the line of least resistance and postpone a matter, however urgent, if it is likely to make him unpopular. It is therefore quite natural if the politically-minded Hindu regards this book as a nuisance. The book treads heavily on the toes of the Arya Samajists. My conclusions have come in sharp conflict with their ideology at two most important points. The Arya Samajists believe that the four Varnas of the Indo-Aryan society have been in existence from the very beginning. The book shows that there was a time when there were only three Varnas in the Indo-Aryan society. The Arya Samajists believe that the Vedas are eternal and sacrosanct. The book shows that portions of the Vedas at any rate, particularly the Purusha Sukta, which is the mainstay of the Arya Samajists, are fabrications by Brahmins intended to serve their own purposes. Both these conclusions are bound to act like atomic bombs on the dogmas of the Arya Samajists. I am not sorry for this clash with Arya Samajists. The Arya Samajists have done great mischief in making the Hindu society a stationary society by preaching that the Vedas are eternal, without beginning, without end, and infallible, and that the social institutions of the Hindus being based on the Vedas are also eternal, without beginning, without end, infallible and therefore requiring no change.

To be permeated with such a belief is the worst thing that can happen to a community. I am convinced that the Hindu society will not accept the necessity of reforming itself unless and until this Arya Samajists' ideology is completely destroyed. The book does render this service, if no other. What the Orthodox Hindu will say about this book I can well imagine for I have been battling with him all these years. The only thing I did not know was how the meek "and non-violent looking Hindu can be violent when anybody attacks his Sacred Books. I became aware of it as never before when last year I received a shower of letters from angry Hindus, who became quite unbalanced by my speech on the subject delivered in Madras. The letters were full of filthy abuse, unmentionable and unprintable, and full of dire threats to my life. Last time they treated me as a first offender and let me off with mere threats. I don't know what they will do this time. For on reading the book they are sure to find more cause for anger at what in their eyes is a repetition of the offence in an aggravated form for having brought forth chapter and verse to show that what goes by the name of Sacred Books contains fabrications which are political in their motive, partisan in their composition and fraudulent in their purpose.

I do not propose to take any notice of their vilifications or their threats. For I know very well that they are a base crew who, professing to defend their religion, have made religion a matter of trade. They are more selfish than any other set of beings in the world, and are prostituting their intelligence to support the vested interests of their class. It is a matter of no small surprise that when the mad dogs of orthodoxy are let loose against a person who has the courage to raise his voice against the so-called Sacred Books of the Hindus, eminent Hindus occupying lofty places, claiming themselves to be highly educated and who could be expected to have no interest and to have a free and open mind become partisans and join the outcry. Even Hindu Judges of High Courts and Hindu Prime Ministers of Indian States do not hesitate to join their kind. They go further. They not only lead the howl against him but even join in the hunt. What is outrageous is that they do so because they believe that their high stations in life would invest their words with an amount of terror which would be sufficient enough to cow down any and every opponent of orthodoxy.

What I would like to tell these amiable gentlemen is that they will not be able to stop me by their imprecations. They do not seem to be aware of the profound and telling words of Dr. Johnson who when confronted with analogous situation said, 'I am not going to be deterred from catching a cheat by the menaces of a ruffian.' I do not wish to be rude to these high placed critics, much less do I want to say that they are playing the part of a ruffian interested in the escape of a cheat. But I do want to tell them two things: firstly that I propose, no matter what happens, to follow the determination of Dr. Johnson in the pursuit of historical truth by the exposure of the Sacred Books so that the Hindus may know that it is the doctrines contained in their Sacred Books which are responsible for the decline and fall of their country and their society; secondly, if the Hindus of this generation do not take notice of what I have to say I am sure the future generation will. I do not despair of success. For I take consolation in the words of the poet Bhavabhuti who said, "Time is infinite and earth is vast, some day there will be born a man who will appreciate what I have said." Whatever that be the book is a challenge to orthodoxy. The only class of Hindus, who are likely to welcome the book are those who believe in the necessity and urgency of social reform.

The fact that it is a problem which will certainly take a long time to solve and will call the efforts of many generations to come, is in their opinion, no justification for postponing the study of that problem. Even an ardent Hindu politician, if he is honest, will admit that the problems arising out of the malignant form of communalism, which is inherent in the Hindu social organization and which the politically minded Hindus desire to ignore or postpone, invariably return to plague those very politicians at every turn. These problems are not the difficulties of the moment. They are our permanent difficulties, that is to say, difficulties of every moment. I am glad to know that such a class of Hindus exists. Small though they be, they are my mainstay and it is to them that I have addressed my argument. It will be said that I have shown no respect for the sacred literature of the Hindus which every sacred literature deserves. If the charge be true, I can plead two circumstances in justification of myself.

Firstly I claim that in my research I have been guided by the best tradition of the historian who treats all literature as vulgar—I am using the word in its original sense of belonging to the people—to be examined and tested by accepted rules of evidence without recognizing any distinction between the sacred and the profane and with the sole object of finding the truth. If in following this tradition I am found wanting in respect and reverence for the sacred literature of the Hindus my duty as a scholar must serve as my excuse. Secondly, respect and reverence for the sacred literature cannot be made to order. They are the results of social factors which make such sentiments natural in one case and quite unnatural in another. Respect and reverence for the sacred literature of the Hindus is natural to a Brahmin scholar. But it is quite unnatural in a non-Brahmin scholar. The explanation of this difference is quite simple. That a Brahmin scholar should treat this sacred literature with uncritical reverence and forbear laying on it the heavy hands which the detachment of an intellectual as distinguished from the merely educated is what is to be expected. For what is this sacred literature? It is a literature which is almost entirely the creation of the Brahmins. Secondly, its whole object is to sustain the superiority and privileges of the Brahmins as against the non-Brahmins. Why should not the Brahmins uphold the sanctity of such a literature? The very reason that leads the Brahmin to uphold it makes the non-Brahmin hate it. Knowing that what is called the sacred literature contains an abominable social philosophy which is responsible for their social degradation, the non-Brahmin reacts to it in a manner quite opposite to that of the Brahmin. That I should be wanting in respect and reverence for the sacred literature of the Hindus should not surprise any one if it is borne in mind that I am a non-Brahmin, not even a non-Brahmin but an Untouchable. My antipathy to the sacred literature could not naturally be less than that of the non-Brahmin. As Prof. Thorndyke says: that a man thinks is a biological fact what he thinks is a sociological fact.

I am aware that this difference in the attitude of a Brahmin scholar and a non-Brahmin scholar towards this sacred literature— literature which is the main source of the material for the study of the problems of the social history of the Hindus— the former with his attitude of uncritical commendation and the latter with his attitude of unsparing condemnation is most harmful to historical research. The mischief done by the Brahmin scholars to historical research is obvious. The Brahmin scholar has a two-fold interest in the maintenance of the sanctity of this literature. In the first place being the production of his forefathers his filial duty leads him to defend it even at the cost of truth. In the second place as it supports the privileges of the Brahmins, he is careful not to do anything which would undermine its authority. The necessity of upholding the system by which he knows he stands to profit, as well as of upholding the prestige of his forefathers as the founders of the system, acts as a silent immaculate premise which is ever present in the mind of the Brahmin scholar and prevents him from reaching or preaching the truth. That is why one finds so little that is original in the field of historical research by Brahmin scholars unless it be a matter of fixing dates or tracing genealogies. The non-Brahmin scholar has none of these limitations and is therefore free to engage himself in a relentless pursuit of truth. That such a difference exists between the two classes of students is not a mere matter of speculation.

This very book is an illustration in point. It contains an exposure of the real character of the conspiracy against the Shudras, which no Brahmin scholar could have had the courage to present. While it is true that a non-Brahmin scholar is free from the inhibitions of the Brahmin scholar he is likely to go to the other extreme and treat the whole literature as a collection of fables and fictions fit to be thrown on the dung heap not worthy of serious study. This is not the spirit of an historian. As has been well said, an historian ought to be exact, sincere, and impartial; free from passion, unbiased by interest, fear, resentment or affection; and faithful to the truth, which is the mother of history, the preserver of great actions, the enemy of oblivion, the witness of the past, the director of the future. In short he must have an open mind, though it may not be an empty mind, and readiness to examine all evidence even though it be spurious. The non-Brahmin scholar may find it difficult to remain true to this spirit of the historian. He is likely to import the spirit of non-Brahmin politics in the examination of the truth or falsity of the ancient literature which is not justifiable. I feel certain that in my research I have kept myself free from such prejudice. In writing about the Shudras I have had present in my mind no other consideration except that of pure history.

It is well-known that there is a non-Brahmin movement in this country which is a political movement of the Shudras. It is also well-known that I have been connected with it. But I am sure that the reader will find that I have not made this book a preface to non-Brahmin politics. I am sensible of the many faults in the presentation of the matter. The book is loaded with quotations, too long and too many. The book is not a work of art and it is possible that readers will find it tedious to go through it. But this fault is not altogether mine. Left to myself, I would have very willingly applied the pruning knife. But the book is written for the ignorant and the uninformed Shudras, who do not know how they came to be what they are.

They do not care how artistically the theme is handled. All they desire is a full harvest of material—the bigger the better.

Those of them to whom I have shown the manuscript have insisted upon retaining the quotations. Indeed, their avidity for such material was so great that some of them went to the length of insisting that besides giving translations in English in the body of the book I should also add the original Sanskrit texts in an Appendix. While I had to deny their request for the reproduction of the original Sanskrit texts, I could not deny their request for retaining the translations on the ground that the material is not readily available to them. When one remembers that it is the Shudras, who have largely been instrumental in sustaining the infamous system of Chaturvarnya, though it has been the primary cause of their degradation and that only the Shudras can destroy the Chaturvarnya, it would be easy to realize why I allowed the necessity of educating and thereby preparing the Shudra fully for such a sacred task to outweigh all other considerations which favoured the deletion or if not deletion the abridgement of the quotations. There are three persons to whom I owe my thanks.

Firstly to the writer of Adhyaya LX of the Shanti Parva of the Mahabharata. Whether it is Vyasa, Vaishampayana, Suta, Lomaharshana or Bhrigu it is difficult to say. But whoever he was, he has rendered great service by giving a full description of Paijavana. If he had not described Paijavana as a Shudra, the clue to the origin of the Shudra would have been completely lost. I express my gratitude to the writer for having preserved so important a piece of information for posterity. Without it, this book could not have been written. Secondly, I must thank Prof. Kangle of Ismail Yusuf College, Andheri, Bombay. He has come to my rescue and has checked the translation of Sanskrit shlokas which occur in the book. As I am not a Sanskrit scholar, his help has been to me a sort of an assurance that I have not bungled badly in dealing with the material which is in Sanskrit. The fact that he has helped me does not mean that he is responsible for such faults and errors as may be discovered by my critics. Thanks are also due to Prof. Manohar Chitnis of the Siddharth College, Bombay, who has been good enough to prepare the Index. I am grateful to Messrs. Charles Scribner's Sons Publishers, New York for their kind permission to reproduce the three maps from Mr. Madison Grant's Passing of the Great Race and which form Appendices II, III and IV of this book.

B. R. AMBEDKAR
"RAJGRAHA," DADAR,
BOMBAY
10th October 1946

The Untouchables

Preface[ix]

This book is a sequel to my treatise called The Shudras—Who they were and How they came to be the Fourth Varna of the Indo-Aryan Society which was published in 1946. Besides the Shudras, the Hindu Civilization has produced three social classes whose existence has not received the attention it deserves. The three classes are :- (i) The Criminal Tribes who number about 20 millions or so; (ii) The Aboriginal Tribes who number about 15 millions; and (iii) The Untouchables who number about 50 millions. The existence of these classes is an abomination. The Hindu Civilization, gauged in the light of these social products, could hardly be called civilization. It is a diabolical contrivance to suppress and enslave humanity. Its proper name would be infamy. What else can be said of a civilization which has produced a mass of people who are taught to accept crime as an approved means of earning their livelihood, another mass of people who are left to live in full bloom of their primitive barbarism in the midst of civilization and a third mass of people who are treated as an entity beyond human intercourse and whose mere touch is enough to cause pollution? In any other country the existence of these classes would have led to searching of the heart and to investigation of their origin. But neither of these has occurred to the mind of the Hindu. The reason is simple. The Hindu does not regard the existence of these classes as a matter of apology or shame and feels no responsibility either to atone for it or to inquire into its origin and growth. On the other hand, every Hindu is taught to believe that his civilization is not only the most ancient but that it is also in many respects altogether unique. No Hindu ever feels tired of repeating these claims. That the Hindu Civilization is the most ancient, one can understand and even allow. But it is not quite so easy to understand on what grounds they rely for claiming that the Hindu Civilization is a unique one. The Hindus may not like it, but so far as it strikes non-Hindus, such a claim can rest only on one ground. It is the existence of these classes for which the Hindu Civilization is responsible. That the existence of such classes is a unique phenomenon, no Hindu need repeat, for nobody can deny the fact. One only wishes that the Hindu realized that it was a matter for which there was more cause for shame than pride.

The inculcation of these false beliefs in the sanity, superiority and sanctity of Hindu Civilization is due entirely to the peculiar social psychology of Hindu scholars. To-day all scholarship is confined to the Brahmins. But unfortunately no Brahmin scholar has so far come forward to play the part of a Voltaire who had the intellectual honesty to rise against the doctrines of the Catholic Church in which he was brought up; nor is one likely to appear on the scene in the future. It is a grave reflection on the scholarship of the Brahmins that they should not have produced a Voltaire. This will not cause surprise if it is remembered that the Brahmin scholar is only a learned man. He is not an intellectual. There is a world of difference between one who is learned and one who is an intellectual. The former is class conscious and is alive to the interests of his class.

The latter is an emancipated being who is free to act without being swayed by class considerations. It is because the Brahmins have been only learned men that they have not produced a Voltaire. Why have the Brahmins not produced a Voltaire? The question can be answered only by another question. Why did the Sultan of Turkey not abolish the religion of the Mohammedan World? Why has no Pope denounced Catholicism? Why has the British Parliament not made a law ordering the killing of all blue-eyed babies? The reason why the Sultan or the Pope or the British Parliament has not done these things is the same as why the Brahmins have not been able to produce a Voltaire. It must be recognized that the selfish interest of a person or of the class to which he belongs always acts as an internal limitation which regulates the direction of his intellect.

The power and position which the Brahmins possess is entirely due to the Hindu Civilization which treats them as supermen and subjects the lower classes to all sorts of disabilities so that they may never rise and challenge or threaten the superiority of the Brahmins over them. As is natural, every Brahmin is interested in the maintenance of Brahmanic supremacy be he orthodox or unorthodox, be he a priest or a grahastha, be he a scholar or not. How can the Brahmins afford to be Voltaires? A Voltaire among the Brahmins would be a positive danger to the maintenance of a civilization which is contrived to maintain Brahmanic supremacy. The point is that the intellect of a Brahmin scholar is severely limited by anxiety to preserve his interest. He suffers from this internal limitation as a result of which he does not allow his intellect full play which honesty and integrity demands. For, he fears that it may affect the interests of his class and therefore his own. But what annoys one is the intolerance of the Brahmin scholar towards any attempt to expose the Brahmanic literature. He himself would not play the part of an iconoclast even where it is necessary. And he would not allow such non-Brahmins as have the capacity to do so to play it. If any non-Brahmin were to make such an attempt the Brahmin scholars would engage in a conspiracy of silence, take no notice of him, condemn him outright on some flimsy grounds or dub his work useless. As a writer engaged in the exposition of the Brahmanic literature I have been a victim of such mean tricks. Notwithstanding the attitude of the Brahmin scholars, I must pursue the task I have undertaken.

For the origin of these classes is a subject which still awaits investigation. This book deals with one of these unfortunate classes namely, the Untouchables. The Untouchables are the most numerous of the three. Their existence is also the most unnatural. And yet there has so far been no investigation into their origin. That the Hindus should not have undertaken such an investigation is perfectly understandable. The old orthodox Hindu does not think that there is anything wrong in the observance of Untouchability. To him it is a normal and natural thing. As such it neither calls for expiation nor explanation. The new modern Hindu realizes the wrong. But he is ashamed to discuss it in public for fear of letting the foreigner know that Hindu Civilization can be guilty of such a vicious and infamous system or social code as evidenced by Untouchability. But what is strange is that Untouchability should have failed to attract the attention of the European student of social institutions. It is difficult to understand why. The fact, however, is there. This book may therefore, be taken as a pioneer attempt in the exploration of a field so completely neglected by everybody.

The book, if I may say so, deals not only with every aspect of the main question set out for inquiry, namely, the origin of Untouchability, but it also deals with almost all questions connected with it. Some of the questions are such that very few people are even aware of them; and those who are aware of them are puzzled by them and do not know how to answer them. To mention only a few, the book deals with such questions as : Why do the Untouchables live outside the village? Why did beef-eating give rise to Untouchability ? Did the Hindus never eat beef ? Why did non-Brahmins give up beef-eating ? What made the Brahmins become vegetarians, etc.? To each one of these, the book suggests an answer. It may be that the answers given in the book to these questions are not all-embracing. Nonetheless it will be found that the book points to a new way of looking at old things. The thesis on the origin of Untouchability advanced in the book is an altogether novel thesis. It comprises the following propositions :- (1) There is no racial difference between the

Hindus and the Untouchables; (2) The distinction between the Hindus and Untouchables in its original form, before the advent of Untouchability, was the distinction between Tribesmen and Broken Men from alien Tribes. It is the Broken Men who subsequently came to be treated as Untouchables; (3) Just as Untouchability has no racial basis so also has it no occupational basis; (4) There are two roots from which Untouchability has sprung: (a) Contempt and hatred of the Broken Men as of Buddhists by the Brahmins: (b) Continuation of beef-eating by the Broken Men after it had been given up by others. (5) In searching for the origin of Untouchability care must be taken to distinguish the Untouchables from the Impure. All orthodox Hindu writers have identified the Impure with the Untouchables. This is an error. Untouchables are distinct from the Impure. (6) While the Impure as a class came into existence at the time of the Dharma Sutras the Untouchables came into being much later than 400 A.D. These conclusions are the result of such historical research as I have been able to make.

The ideal which a historian should place before himself has been well defined by Goethe who said[x]: "The historian's duty is to separate the true from the false, the certain from the uncertain, and the doubtful from that which cannot be accepted ... ... Every investigator must before all things look upon himself as one who is summoned to serve on a jury. He has only to consider how far the statement of the case is complete and clearly set forth by the evidence. Then he draws his conclusion and gives his vote, whether it be that his opinion coincides with that of the foreman or not." There can be no difficulty in giving effect to Goethe's direction when the relevant and necessary facts are forthcoming. All this advice is of course very valuable and very necessary. But Goethe does not tell what the historian is to do when he comes across a missing link, when no direct evidence of connected relations between important events is available.

I mention this because in the course of my investigations into the origin of Untouchability and other inter connected problems I have been confronted with many missing links. It is true that I am not the only one who has been confronted with them. All students of ancient Indian history have had to face them. For as Mount Stuart Elphinstone has observed in Indian history "no date of a public event can be fixed before the invasion of Alexander: and no connected relation of the natural transactions can be attempted until after the Mohamedan conquest." This is a sad confession but that again does not help.

 The question is: "What is a student of history to do? Is he to cry halt and stop his work until the link is discovered?" I think not. I believe that in such cases it is permissible for him to use his imagination and intuition to bridge the gaps left in the chain of facts by links not yet discovered and to propound a working hypothesis suggesting how facts which cannot be connected by known facts might have been inter-connected. I must admit that rather than hold up the work, I have preferred to resort to this means to get over the difficulty created by the missing links which have come in my way. Critics may use this weakness to condemn the thesis as violating the canons of historical research. If such be the attitude of the critics I must remind them that if there is a law which governs the evaluation of the results of historical results then refusal to accept a thesis on the ground that it is based on direct evidence is bad law. Instead of concentrating themselves on the issue of direct evidence versus inferential evidence and inferential evidence versus speculation, what the critics should concern themselves with is to examine (i) whether the thesis is based on pure conjecture, and (ii) whether the thesis is possible and if so does it fit in with facts better than mine does?

On the first issue I could say that the thesis would not be unsound merely because in some parts it is based on guess.

My critics should remember that we are dealing with an institution the origin of which is lost in antiquity. The present attempt to explain the origin of Untouchability is not the same as writing history from texts which speak with certainty. It is a case of reconstructing history where there are no texts, and if there are, they have no direct bearing on the question. In such circumstances what one has to do is to strive to divine what the texts conceal or suggest without being even quite certain of having found the truth. The task is one of gathering survivals of the past, placing them together and making them tell the story of their birth. The task is analogous to that of the archaeologist who constructs a city from broken stones or of the palaeontologist who conceives an extinct animal from scattered bones and teeth or of a painter who reads the lines of the horizon and the smallest vestiges on the slopes of the hill to make up a scene. In this sense the book is a work of art even more than of history. The origin of Untouchability lies buried in a dead past which nobody knows.

To make it alive is like an attempt to reclaim to history a city which has been dead since ages past and present it as it was in its original condition. It cannot but be that imagination and hypothesis should pay a large part in such a work. But that in itself cannot be a ground for the condemnation of the thesis. For without trained imagination no scientific inquiry can be fruitful and hypothesis is the very soul of science. As Maxim Gorky has said[xi]: "Science and literature have much in common; in both, observation, comparison and study are of fundamental importance; the artist like the scientist, needs both imagination and intuition. Imagination and intuition bridge the gaps in the chain of facts by its as yet undiscovered links and permit the scientist to create hypothesis and theories which more or less correctly and successfully direct the searching of the mind in its study of the forms and phenomenon of nature. They are of literary creation; the art of creating characters and types demands imagination, intuition, the ability to make things up in one's own mind". It is therefore unnecessary for me to apologize for having resorted to constructing links where they were missing. Nor can my thesis be said to be vitiated on that account for nowhere is the construction of links based on pure conjecture.

The thesis in great part is based on facts and inferences from facts. And where it is not based on facts or inferences from facts, it is based on circumstantial evidence of presumptive character resting on considerable degree of probability. There is nothing that I have urged in support of my thesis which I have asked my readers to accept on trust. I have at least shown that there exists a preponderance of probability in favour of what I have asserted. It would be nothing but pedantry to say that a preponderance of probability is not a sufficient basis for a valid decision. On the second point with the examination of which, I said, my critics should concern themselves what I would like to say is that I am not so vain as to claim any finality for my thesis.

I do not ask them to accept it as the last word. I do not wish to influence their judgement. They are of course free to come to their own conclusion. All I say to them is to consider whether this thesis is not a workable and therefore, for the time being, a valid hypothesis if the test of a valid hypothesis is that it should fit in with all surrounding facts, explain them and give them a meaning which in its absence they do not appear to have. I do not want anything more from my critics than a fair and unbiased appraisal.

B. R. AMBEDKAR
January 1, 1948
1, Hardinge Avenue,
New Delhi

Essays on Untouchable and Untouchability

Preface[xii]

It is usual to hear all those who feel moved by the deplorable condition of the Untouchables unburden themselves by uttering the cry "We must do something for the Untouchables". One seldom hears any of the persons interested in the problem saying 'Let us do something to change the Touchable Hindu'. It is invariably assumed that the object to be reclaimed is the Untouchables. If there is to be a Mission, it must be to the Untouchables and if the Untouchables can be cured, untouchability will vanish. Nothing requires to be done to the Touchable. He is sound in mind, manners and morals. He is whole, there is nothing wrong with him. Is this assumption correct ? Whether correct or not, the Hindus like to cling to it. The assumption has the supreme merit of satisfying themselves that they are not responsible for the problem of the Untouchables.

How natural is such an attitude is illustrated by the attitude of the Gentile towards the Jews. Like the Hindus the Gentiles also do not admit that the Jewish problem is in essence a Gentile problem. The observations of Louis Goulding on the subject are therefore very illuminating. In order to show how the Jewish problem is in its essence a Gentile problem, he says:

> "I beg leave to give a very homely instance
> of the sense in which I consider the Jewish
> Problem in essence a Gentile Problem. A
> close acquaintance of mine is a certain Irish
> terrier of mixed pedigree, the dog Paddy,
> who is to my friend John Smith as the apple
> of both his eyes. Paddy dislikes Scotch

terriers; it is enough for one to pass within twenty yards of Paddy to deafen the neighbourhood with challenges and insults. It is a practice which John Smith deplores, which, therefore, he does his best to check—all the more as the objects of Paddy's detestation are often inoffensive creatures, who seldom speak first. Despite all his affection for Paddy, he considers, as I do, that Paddy's unmannerly behaviour is due to some measure of original sin in Paddy. It has not yet been suggested to us that what is here involved is a Scotch Terrier Problem and that when Paddy attacks a neighbour who is peacefully engaged in inspecting the evening smells it is the neighbour who should be arraigned for inciting to attack by the fact of his existence."

There is here a complete analogy between the Jewish Problem and the problem of the Untouchables. What Paddy is to the Scotch Terrier, the Gentile is to the Jews, and the Hindu is to the Untouchables. But there is one aspect in which the Jewish Problem stands in contrast to the Gentile Problem. The Jews and the Gentiles are separated by an antagonism of the creeds. The Jewish creed is opposed to that of the Gentile creed. The Hindus and the Untouchables are not separated by any such antagonism. They have a common creed and observe the same cults.

The second explanation is that the Jews wish to remain separate from the Gentiles. While the first explanation is chauvinistic the second seems to be founded on historical truth. Many attempts have been made in the past by the Gentiles to assimilate the Jews. But the Jews have always resisted them. Two instances of this may be referred.

The first instance relates to the Napoleonic regime. After the National Assembly of France had agreed to the declaration of the 'Rights of man' to the Jews, the Jewish question was again reopened by the guild merchants and religious reactionaries of Alsace. Napoleon resolved to submit the question to the consideration of the Jews themselves. He convened an Assembly of Jewish Notables of France, Germany and Italy in order to ascertain whether the principles of Judaism were compatible with the requirements of citizenship as he wished to fuse the Jewish element with the dominant population. The Assembly consisting of 111 deputies, met in the Town Hall of Paris on the 25th of July 1806, and was required to frame replies to twelve questions relating mainly to the possibility of Jewish patriotism, the permissibility of inter-marriage between Jew and Non-Jew, and the legality of usury. So pleased was Napoleon with the pronouncements of the Assembly that he summoned a Sanhedrin after the model of the ancient council of Jerusalem to convert them into the decree of a Legislative body. The Sanhedrin, comprising of 71 deputies from France, Germany, Holland and Italy met under the presidency of Rabbi Sinzheim, of Strassburg on 9th February 1807, and adopted a sort of Charter which exhorted the Jews to look upon France as their fatherland, to regard its citizens as their brethren, and to speak its language, and which also pressed toleration of marriages between Jews and Christians while declaring that they could not be sanctioned by the synagogue. It will be noted that the Jews refused to sanction inter marriages between Jews and non-Jews. They only agreed to tolerate them.

The second instance relates to what happened when the Batavian Republic was established in 1795. The more energetic members of the Jewish community pressed for a removal of the many disabilities under which they laboured. But the demand for the fuller rights of citizenship made by the progressive Jews was at first, strangely enough, opposed by the leaders of the Amsterdam community, who feared that civil equality would militate against the conservation of Judaism and declared that their co-religionists renounced their rights of citizenship in obedience to the dictates of their faith. This shows that the Jews preferred to live as strangers rather than as members of the community.

Whatever the value of their explanations the Gentiles have at least realized that there rests upon them a responsibility to show cause for their unnatural attitude towards the Jews. The Hindu has never realised this responsibility of justifying his treatment of the Untouchables. The responsibility of the Hindus is much greater because there is no plausible explanation he can offer in justification of untouchability. He cannot say that the Untouchable is a leper or a mortal wretch who must be shunned. He cannot say that between him and the Untouchables, there is a gulf due to religious antagonism which is not possible to bridge. Nor can he plead that it is the Untouchable who does not wish to assimilate with the Hindus.

But that is not the case with the Untouchables. They too are in a different sense an eternal people who are separate from the rest. But this separateness, their segregation is not the result of their wish. They are punished not because they do not want to mix. They are punished because they want to be one with the Hindus. In other words, though the problem of the Jews and of the Untouchables is similar in nature— inasmuch as the problem is created by others—it is essentially different. The Jew's case is one of the voluntary isolation. The case of the Untouchables is that of compulsory segregation. Untouchability is an infliction and not a choice.

Untouchable Workers of Bombay City

A book by G. R. Pradhan, Ph.D.

Foreword[xiii]

This treatise is a thesis which the author wrote in fulfilment of the requirements prescribed by the University of Bombay for the degree of Doctor of Philosophy in Arts. That was as accepted by the University, should constitute sufficient recommendation in favour of its merits and no such thing as a Foreword from me should have been thought necessary by the Author. I do not know why the Author feels the necessity of a word from me. Probably, that I do from the community whose life has been the subject-matter of this investigation is the reason which has led him to call upon me to write a Foreword and I gladly respond to his invitation.

The author has studied the life of the Untouchables in the City of Bombay under various heads and thus gives quantitative idea of the extent of the overcrowding, the earnings, employment, debts, etc. that prevails among the Untouchables. He has collected data which is certainly valuable. In any statistical investigation the question that arises is whether the cases studied are typical or not. The average to be normal, the cases investigated must be typical. There is no reason to suppose that his cases are not typical. It may, therefore, be taken that the picture of the life of the Untouchables he has given, is a true picture.

This study would have been of greater value if it had been a comparative study contrasting the social condition of the Untouchables with that of the Caste-Hindus. But that it is not. Such a study was all the more necessary in view of the opinion on the one hand and caste Hindus on the other, if it is proved that the Untouchable does not suffer by reason of his Untouchability. But if on comparison it is found that the Untouchable suffers in his earning, in his employment and in other respects in a competitive society as against a caste Hindu and if this disadvantage is attributable to no factor other than Untouchability, then it will have to be admitted that the case for conversion was strong. But all that must await as comparative study. Such a study will have to be undertaken someday either by the author of this book or by someone else if the present study is to be a useful guide for understanding why the conclusions drawn by the author are what they are; and whether the differences if any in the condition of the touchables and Untouchables is due to any such social factor as Untouchability. As a preliminary to such an effort the booklet must be welcomed.

B. R. Ambedkar
Rajgrah, Dadar
10-2-1938

PART 5 POLITICAL

Dr Ambedkar was a prolific writer on politics, both in terms of its theory and practice. One of his notable talks was 'Ranade, Gandhi and Jinnah,' which he delivered on Justice MG Ranade's birthday. In this talk, he expressed his views on Hero worship and nationalism, which were ahead of his time. Although the purpose of his talk was to celebrate Ranade's birthday, he used the opportunity to raise issues that are still relevant today. Additionally, the preface of 'What Congress and Gandhi had done to the Untouchables,' Thoughts on Pakistan, and Thoughts on Linguistic States are included in this section. It is interesting to note that in 1955, Dr Ambedkar proposed the division of larger states into smaller ones, with Jharkhand, Uttarakhand, Chhattisgarh, and Telangana being professed by him.

Ranade, Gandhi and Jinnah

The Deccan Sabha of Poona invited me to deliver an address on the 101st birthday of the late Justice Mahadev Govind Ranade which it proposed to celebrate and which fell on the 18th January 1940. I was not very willing to accept the invitation. For I knew that my views on social and political problems, a discussion of which could not be avoided in a discourse on Ranade, would not be very pleasing to the audience and even perhaps to the members of the Deccan Sabha. In the end, I accepted their invitation. At the time when I delivered the address, I had no intention of publishing it. Addresses delivered on anniversaries of great men are generally occasional pieces. They do not have much permanent value. I did not think that my address was an exception to this. But I have some troublesome friends who have been keen on seeing the whole of it in print and have been insisting upon it.

I am indifferent to the idea. I am quite content with the publicity it has received and I have no desire to seek more. At the same time if there are people who think that it is worthy of being rescued from falling into oblivion, I do not see any reason for disappointing them. The address as printed differs from the address as delivered in two respects. Section X of the address was omitted from the address as delivered to prevent the performance going beyond reasonable time. Even without it, it took one hour and a half to deliver the address. This is one difference. The other difference lies in the omission of a large portion of Section VIII which was devoted to a comparison of Ranade with Phule. For the omission there are two reasons. In the first place, the comparison was not sufficiently full and detailed to do justice to the two men ; in the second place, when the difficulties of finding enough paper compelled me to sacrifice some portion of the address this appeared to be best offering.

The publication of the address is taking place under peculiar circumstances. Ordinarily, reviews follow publication. In this case the situation is reversed. What is worse is that the reviews have condemned the address in scathing terms. This is a matter primarily for the publishers to worry about. I am happy that the publisher knows the risk and he takes it. Nothing more need be said about it except that it supports the view taken by my friends that the address contains matter which is of more than ephemeral value. As for myself I am not in the least perturbed by the condemnation of this address by the Press. What is the ground for its condemnation ? And who has come forward to condemn it ? I am condemned because I criticized Mr. Gandhi and Mr. Jinnah for the mess they have made of Indian politics, and that in doing so I am alleged to have shown towards them hatred and disrespect. In reply to this charge what I have to say is that I have been a critic and I must continue to be such. It may be I am making mistakes but I have always felt that it is better to make mistakes than to accept guidance and direction from others or to sit silent and allow things to deteriorate.

Those who have accused me of having been actuated by feelings of hatred forget two things. In the first place this alleged hatred is not born of anything that can be called personal. If I am against them it is because I want a settlement. I want a settlement of some sort and I am not prepared to wait for an ideal settlement. Nor can I tolerate anyone on whose will and consent settlement depends to stand on dignity and play the Grand Moghul. In the second place, no one can hope to make any effective mark upon his time and bring the aid that is worth bringing to great principles and struggling causes if he is not strong in his love and his hatred.

I hate injustice, tyranny, pompousness and humbug, and my hatred embraces all those who are guilty of them. I want to tell my critics that I regard my feelings of hatred as a real force. They are only the reflex of the love I bear for the causes I believe in and I am in no wise ashamed of it. For these reasons I tender no apology for my criticism of Mr. Gandhi and Mr. Jinnah, the two men who have brought India's political progress to a standstill. The condemnation is by the Congress Press. I know the Congress Press well. I attach no value to its criticism. It has never refuted my arguments. It knows only to criticise, rebuke and revile me for everything I do and to misreport, misrepresent and pervert everything I say. Nothing, that I do, pleases the Congress Press. This animosity of the Congress Press towards me can to my mind not unfairly, be explained as a reflex of the hatred of the Hindus for the Untouchables. That their animosity has become personal is clear from the fact that the Congress Press feels offended for my having criticised Mr. Jinnah who has been the butt and the target of the Congress for the last several years.

However strong and however filthy be the abuses which the Congress Press chooses to shower on me I must do my duty. I am no worshipper of idols. I believe in breaking them. I insist that if I hate Mr. Gandhi and Mr. Jinnah—I dislike them, I do not hate them—it is because I love India more. That is the true faith of a nationalist. I have hopes that my countrymen, will someday learn that the country is greater

than the men, that the worship of Mr. Gandhi or Mr. Jinnah
and service to India are two very different things and may
even be contradictory of each other.

B. R. AMBEDKAR
22 Prithviraj Road
New Delhi
15th March 1943

Federation versus Freedom

Preface[xv]

A word or two as regards the origin of this tract and the motive which has led me to publish it at this time will, I think, not be out of place. Many in this country must be aware that there exists in Poona an institution which is called the Gokhale Institute of Politics and Economics, working under the direction of Dr. D. R. Gadgil. The Institute holds a function annually to celebrate what is called the Founder's Day and invites someone to deliver an address on some subject connected with politics or economics. This year, I was asked by Dr. Gadgil to deliver an address. I accepted the invitation and chose the Federal Scheme as the subject of my address. The address covered both (1) the structure of the Federation and (2) a critique of that structure.

The address was delivered on 29th January 1939 at the Gokhale Hall in Poona. The address as prepared had become too lengthy for the time allotted to me and although I kept the audience for two hours when usually the time allotted for such address is one hour I had to omit from the address the whole of the part relating to the Federal structure and some portion from the part relating to the criticism of the structure. This tract, however, contains the whole of the original address prepared by me for the occasion. So much for the origin of this tract.Now as to the reasons for publishing it. All addresses delivered at the Gokhale Institute are published. It is in the course of things that this also should be published. But there are other reasons besides this, which have prevailed with me to publish it. So far as the Federation is concerned, the generality of the Indian public seems to be living in a fog. Beyond the fact that there is to be a Federation and that the Federation is a bad thing the general public has no clear conception of what is the nature of this Federation and is, therefore, unable to form an intelligent opinion about it. It is necessary that the general public should have in its hand a leaflet containing an outline of the Federal structure and a criticism of that structure in small compass sufficient to convey a workable understanding of the Scheme.

I feel this Tract will supply this need. I also think that the publication of this tract will be regarded as timely. Federation is a very live issue and it is also a very urgent one. Soon the people of British India will be called upon to decide whether they should accept the Federal Scheme or they should not. The premier political organization in this Country, namely, the Congress seems to be willing to accept this Federation as it has accepted Provincial Autonomy. The negotiations that are going on with the Muslim League and the manoeuvres that are being carried on with the Indian States give me at any rate the impression that the Congress is prepared to accept the Federation and that these negotiations and manoeuvres are designed to bring about a working arrangement with other parties so that with their help the Congress may be in the saddle at the Centre as it has been in the Provinces. Mr. Subhas Chandra Bose has even gone to the length of suggesting that the right wing of the Congress has committed itself to this Federation so far that it has already selected its cabinet. It matters not whether all this is true or not. I hope all this is untrue. Be that as it may, the matter is both grave and urgent, and I think all those who have anything to say on the subject should speak it out. Indeed I feel that silence at such a time will be criminal. That is why I have hastened to publish my address. I believe that I have views on the subject of Federation which even if they do not convince others will at least provoke them to think

B. R. AMBEDKAR
Rajgraha Dadar,
Bombay 14
1-3-39

Pakistan or the Partition of India

Preface[xvi]

The problem of Pakistan has given a headache to everyone, more so to me than to anybody else. I cannot help recalling with regret how much of my time it has consumed when so much of my other literary work of greater importance to me than this is held up for want of it. I therefore hope that this second edition will also be the last. I trust that before it is exhausted either the question will be settled or withdrawn. There are four respects in which this second edition differs from the first. *The first edition contained many misprints which formed the subject of complaints from many readers as well as reviewers. In preparing this edition, I have taken as much care as is possible to leave no room for complaint on this score.

The first edition consisted only of three parts. Part V is an addition. It contains my own views on the various issues involved in the problem of Pakistan. It has been added because of the criticism levelled against the first edition that while I wrote about Pakistan I did not state what views I held on the subject. The present edition differs from the first in another respect. The maps contained in the first edition are retained but the number of appendices have been enlarged. In the first edition there were only eleven appendices. The present edition has twenty-five. To this edition I have also added an index which did not find a place in the first edition. The book appears to have supplied a real want. I have seen how the thoughts, ideas and arguments contained in it have been pillaged by authors, politicians and editors of newspapers to support their sides.

I am sorry they did not observe the decency of acknowledging the source even when they lifted not merely the argument but also the language of the book. But that is a matter I do not mind. I am glad that the book has been of service to * In the first edition there unfortunately occurred through oversight in proof correction a discrepancy between the population figures in the different districts of Bengal and the map showing the lay-out of Pakistan as applied to Bengal which had resulted in two districts which should have been included in the Pakistan area being excluded from it. In this edition, this error has been rectified and the map and the figures have been brought into conformity.

Indians who are faced with this knotty problem of Pakistan. The fact that Mr. Gandhi and Mr. Jinnah in their recent talks cited the book as an authority on the subject which might be consulted with advantage bespeaks the worth of the book. The book by its name might appear to deal only with the X. Y. Z. of Pakistan. It does more than that. It is an analytical presentation of Indian history and Indian politics in their communal aspects. As such, it is intended to explain the A. B. C. of Pakistan also.

The book is more than a mere treatise on Pakistan. The material relating to Indian history and Indian politics contained in this book is so large and so varied that it might well be called Indian Political What is What. The book has displeased both Hindus as well as Muslims though the reasons for the dislike of the Hindus are different from the reasons for the dislike of the Muslims. I am not sorry for this reception given to my book. That it is disowned by the Hindus and unowned by the Muslims is to me the best evidence that it has the vices of neither and that from the point of view of independence of thought and fearless presentation of facts the book is not a party production. Some people are sore because what I have said has hurt them.

I have not, I confess, allowed myself to be influenced by fears of wounding either individuals or classes, or shocking opinions however respectable they may be. I have often felt regret in pursuing this course, but remorse never. Those whom I may have offended must forgive me, in consideration of the honesty and disinterestedness of my aim. I do not claim to have written dispassionately though I trust I have written without prejudice. It would be hardly possible—I was going to say decent—for an Indian to be calm when he talks of his country and thinks of the times. In dealing with the question of Pakistan my object has been to draw a perfectly accurate, and at the same time, a suggestive picture of the situation as I see it. Whatever points of strength and weakness I have discovered on either side I have brought them boldly forward. I have taken pains to throw light on the mischievous effects that are likely to proceed from an obstinate and impracticable course of action.

The witness of history regarding the conflict between the forces of the authority of the State and of anti-State nationalism within, has been uncertain, if not equivocal. As Prof. Friedmann[xvii] observes "There is not a single modern State which has not, at one time or another, forced a recalcitrant national group to live under its authority. Scots, Bretons, Catalans, Germans, Poles, Czechs, Finns, all have, at some time or another, been compelled to accept the authority of a more powerful State whether they liked it or not. Often, as in Great Britain or France, force eventually led to co-operation and a co-ordination of State authority and national cohesion. But in many cases, such as those of Germany, Poland, Italy and a host of Central European and Balkan countries, the forces of Nationalism did not rest until they had thrown off the shackles of State Power and formed a State of their own . . . . . " In the last edition, I depicted the experience of countries in which the State engaged itself in senseless suppression of nationalism and weathered away in the attempt. In this edition I have added by way of contrast

the experience of other countries to show that given the will
to live together it is not impossible for diverse communities
and even for diverse nations to live in the bosom of one
State.

It might be said that in tendering advice to both sides I have
used terms more passionate than they need have been. If I
have done so it is because I felt that the manner of the
physician who tries to surprise the vital principle in each
paralyzed organ in order to goad it to action was best suited
to stir up the average Indian who is complacent if not
somnolent, who is unsuspecting if not ill-informed, to realize
what is happening. I hope my effort will have the desired
effect. I cannot close this preface without thanking Prof.
Manohar B. Chitnis of the Khalsa College, Bombay, and Mr.
K. V. Chitre for their untiring labours to remove all printer's
and clerical errors that had crept into the first edition and to
see that this edition is free from all such blemishes. I am also
very grateful to Prof. Chitnis for the preparation of the Index
which has undoubtedly enhanced the utility of the book.

B. R. AMBEDKAR
1st January 1945,
22, Prithviraj Road,
New Delhi.

PROLOGUE

It can rightly be said that the long introduction with which this treatise opens leaves no excuse for a prologue. But there is an epilogue which is affixed to the treatise. Having done that, I thought of prefixing a prologue, firstly, because an epilogue needs to be balanced by a prologue, and secondly, because the prologue gives me room to state in a few words the origin of this treatise to those who may be curious to know it and to impress upon the readers the importance of the issues raised in it. For the satisfaction of the curious it may be stated that there exists, at any rate in the Bombay Presidency, a political organization called the Independent Labour Party (abbreviated into I.L.P.) for the last three years. It is not an ancient, hoary organization which can claim to have grown grey in politics. The I.L.P. is not in its dotage and is not overtaken by senility, for which second childhood is given as a more agreeable name. Compared with other political organizations, the I.L.P. is a young and fairly active body, not subservient to any clique or interest. Immediately after the passing of the Lahore Resolution on Pakistan by the Muslim League, the Executive Council of the I.L.P. met to consider what attitude it should adopt towards this project of Pakistan. The Executive Council could see that there was underlying Pakistan an idea to which no objection could be taken. Indeed, the Council was attracted to the scheme of Pakistan inasmuch as it meant the creation of ethnic states as a solution of the communal problem. The Council, however, did not feel competent to pronounce at that stage a decided opinion on the issue of Pakistan. The Council, therefore, resolved to appoint a committee to study the question and make a report on it. The committee consisted of myself as the Chairman, and Principal M. V. Donde, B.A.; Mr. S. C. Joshi, M.A., LL.B., Advocate (O.S.), M.L.C.; Mr. R. R. Bhole, B.Sc., LL.B., M.L.A.; Mr. D. G. Jadhav, B.A., LL.B., M.L.A., and Mr. A. V. Chitre, B.A., M.L.A., all belonging to the I.L.P., as members of the committee. Mr. D. V. Pradhan, Member, Bombay Municipal Corporation, acted as Secretary to the committee. The committee asked me to prepare a report on Pakistan which I did. The same was submitted to the Executive Council of the I.L.P., which resolved that the report should be published. The treatise now published is that report.

The book is intended to assist the student of Pakistan to come to his own conclusion. With that object in view, I have not only assembled in this volume all the necessary and relevant data but have also added 14 appendices and 3 maps, which in my judgment, form an important accompaniment to the book. It is not enough for the reader to go over the material collected in the following pages. He must also reflect over it. Let him take to heart the warning which Carlyle gave to Englishmen of his generation. He said: "The Genius of England no longer soars Sunward, world-defiant, like an Eagle through the storms, 'mewing her mighty youth ,'..........
......the Genius of England— much like a greedy Ostrich intent on provender and a whole skin..........; with its Ostrich-head stuck into ...... whatever sheltering Fallacy there may be, and so awaits the issue. The issue has been slow; but it now seems to have been inevitable. No Ostrich, intent on gross terrene provender and sticking its head into Fallacies, but will be awakened one day—in a terrible a posteriori manner if not otherwise! Awake before it comes to that. Gods and men did us awake ! The Voices of our Fathers, with thousandfold stern monition to one and all, bid us awake". This warning, I am convinced, applies to Indians in their present circumstances as it once did to Englishmen, and Indians, if they pay no heed to it, will do so at their peril.

Now, a word for those who have helped me in the preparation of this report. Mr. M. G. Tipnis, D.C.E. (Kalabhuwan, Baroda), and Mr. Chhaganlal S. Mody have rendered me great assistance, the former in preparing the maps and the latter in typing the manuscript. I wish to express my gratitude to both for their work which they have done purely as a labour of love. Thanks are also due in a special measure to my friends Mr. B. R. Kadrekar and Mr. K. V. Chitre for their labours in undertaking the most uninteresting and dull task of correcting the proofs and supervising the printing.

B. R. AMBEDKAR.
Rajagrah, Dadar,
Bombay, 14
28th December, 1940

What Congress and Gandhi had Done to the Untouchables

Preface[xviii]

In 1892, there took place in England a new election to Parliament, in which the Conservatives headed by Lord Salisbury lost and the Liberals headed by Mr. Gladstone won. The remarkable thing about this election was that notwithstanding the defeat of his party at the polls, Lord Salisbury—contrary to Parliamentary convention—refused to surrender his office to the leader of the Liberal Party. When Parliament assembled, the Queen delivered the usual gracious speech from the throne containing the legislative programme of Lord Salisbury's Government and the usual address to Her Majesty was moved from the Government side. Lord Salisbury's Government was an illegitimate Government. It was a challenge to the fundamental principle of the British Constitution, which recognised Parliamentary Majority as the only title deed for a Party's right to form a Government. The Liberals took up the challenge and tabled an amendment to the address. The amendment sought to condemn Lord Salisbury's Government for its insistence on continuing in office, notwithstanding the fact that it had no majority behind it. The task of moving the amendment was entrusted to the late Lord (then Mr.) Asquith. In his speech in support of the amendment, Mr. Asquith used the now famous phrase— "Causafinitaest: Roma locuta est." (Rome has spoken and the dispute must end). The phrase was originally used by St. Augustine but in a different context. It was used in the course of a religious controversy and had come to be used as a foundation for Papal Sovereignty. Mr. Asquith used it as a political maxim embodying the basic principle of Parliamentary Democracy.

Today it is accepted as the fundamental principle on which Popular Government rests, namely, the Right of a Political Majority to Rule. It told instantaneously against Salisbury's Government and must tell against all parties who fail at the polls wherever Parliamentary Democracy is in operation. I was reminded of this maxim when the results of the Elections to the Provincial Legislatures in India, which took place in February 1937 under the Government of India Act, 1935, were announced. Congressmen did not actually say "Causafinitaest: India locuta est." But so far as the parties, which had opposed the Congress in the Elections, were concerned, that is what the results of the Elections seemed to, proclaim. Having led the Untouchables against the Congress: for full five years in the Round Table Conference and in the Joint Parliamentary Committee, I could not pretend to be unaffected by the results of the Elections. To me the question was : Had the Untouchables gone over to the Congress ? Such a thing was to me unimaginable. For, I could not believe that the Untouchables—apart from a few agents of the Congress who are always tempted by the Congress gold to play the part of the traitor—could think of going over to the Congress en masse forgetting how Mr. Gandhi and the Congress opposed, inch by inch up to the very last moment, every one of their demands for political safeguards. I had therefore decided to study the Returns of the election that took place in 1937. While I was convinced that such a study was of great necessity from the point of view of the Untouchables, the work proceeded at a snail's pace. This was due to three causes. The work had to be kept aside for some time to give precedence to other literary projects, the urgency of which demanded a degree of priority which it was not possible to refuse. Secondly, the Blue Book on the Election Results of 1937, which was submitted to Parliament soon after the elections had taken place and which is the primary source for figures regarding the elections, proved inadequate and insufficient for my purpose. It does not give separately figures showing how the Scheduled Castes electors voted and how many votes the Scheduled Caste candidates got. It gives figures showing how electors in different constituencies voted, without making any distinction between Hindu voters and the Scheduled Castes voters. Circular letters had therefore to be issued to the various Provincial Governments requesting them to send me the figures showing distribution of voting by Scheduled Caste electors and the number of votes secured by each Scheduled Caste candidate. This inevitably delayed the work. Thirdly, the examination of these election returns proved a very laborious task as the statistical tables given in the Appendices to this book will show. The work thus lingered on. I regret very much this delay. For I know how much mischief has been done by the Congress during the interval. The Congress has advertised the election results to bolster up its claim to represent the Untouchables. The main point in the advertisement is that out of 151 seats assigned to the Scheduled Castes the Independent Labour Party which was organized by me got only 12 seats and the rest of the seats were captured by the Congress. This mess is served out from the Congress kitchen as conclusive proof to show that the Congress represents the Untouchables.

This false propaganda seems to have gone home in some quarters. Even a man like Mr. H. N. Brailsford has reproduced in his 'Subject India' this absurd Congress version, without any attempt at verification and with apparent acceptance of its truth. I am sure that the results of the elections as set out in this book will hit the nail squarely on the head of this false propaganda. For, the Congress version of the results of the election is an utter perversion. As a matter of fact the results of 1937 Election conclusively disprove the Congress claim to represent the Untouchables. Far from supporting the Congress version the results of the Election show : (1) that out of 151 the Congress got only 73 seats; (2) that the Untouchables in almost every constituency fought against the Congress by putting up their own candidates; (3) that the majority of 73 seats won by the

Congress were won with the help of Hindu votes and they do not therefore in any way represent the Scheduled Castes; and (4) that of 151 seats those won by the Congress in, the real sense i.e., with the majority of votes of the Scheduled Castes, were only 38. As to the Independent Labour Party it was started in 1937 just a few months before the elections. It functioned only in the Province of Bombay. There was no time to organize branches in other Provinces. Elections on the ticket of the Independent Labour Party were fought only in the Province of Bombay and there the Independent Labour Party far from being a failure obtained an astonishing degree of success. Out of the 15 seats assigned to the Scheduled Castes in Bombay Presidency it captured 13 and in addition it won 2 general seats.

I am therefore glad that at long last I have succeeded in completing the work which proves beyond the shadow of doubt that the story that the Congress captured all the seats reserved for the Scheduled Castes and that the Independent Labour Party was a failure, is a wicked lie. I trust that the book will prove interesting and instructive for all those who are interested in the subject and who desire to know the truth. Before closing this preface, I wish to express my gratitude to those from whom I have received assistance in one form or another. I am grateful to the Provincial Governments for the troubles they have taken in responding to my circular and sending me additional facts and figures which I had called for. My thanks are also due to Mr. Karan Singh Kane, B.A., M.L.A., at one time, Parliamentary Secretary in the U. P. Congress Government, for the help he has rendered in the most laborious task of preparing the tables." The reader who reads the above preface and compares it with the table of contents will at once find that the book deals with topics which lie far outside its boundary. The curious may like to know how the foregoing part of the preface is related to the table of contents. The explanation lies in the fact that the book in its present final form is quite different from what it was in its original form. In its original form it covered in very brief compass matter now dealt with on a vastly bigger scale in Chapters IV, V, VI, VII and IX and the statistical appendices. The foregoing part of the preface belonged to the book in its original form. That is why I have put it in inverted commas. The curious may also like to know why the final form of the book came to be so different from the original. The explanation is quite simple. The proofs of the book in its original form were seen by a friend and coworker. He was dissatisfied with the scope of the book and insisted that it is not enough to deal with election results to expose the Congress claim to represent the Untouchables. I must do more.

I must expose the efforts of the Congress and Mr. Gandhi to improve the lot of the Untouchables for the information of the Untouchables and also of the foreigners whom the Congress had deluded into accepting its side by misrepresentation of facts. Besides the difficulties arising out of the fact that the book was already in proof form, this was a tall order and appeared to be beyond me having regard to other claims on my time. He would not, however, give way and I had therefore to accept his plan. The original work which would have been about 75 pages in print had to be completely recast and enlarged. The book in the present form is a complete transformation. It records the deeds of the Congress and Mr. Gandhi from 1917 to date in so far as they touch the problem of the Untouchables. Much is written about the Congress, far more about Mr. Gandhi. But no one has so far told the story of what they have done about the Untouchables. Everyone knows that Mr. Gandhi values more his reputation as the saviour of the Untouchables than his reputation as the champion of Swaraj or as the protagonist of Ahimsa. At the Round Table Conference he claimed to be the sole champion of the Untouchables and was not even prepared to share the honour with anyone else. I remember what a scene he created when his claim was contested. Mr.

Gandhi does not merely claim for himself the championship of the Untouchables. He claims similar championship for the Congress. The Congress, he says, is fully pledged to redress the wrongs done to the Untouchables and argues that any attempt to give political safeguards to the Untouchables is unnecessary and harmful. It is therefore a great pity that no detailed study of these claims by Mr. Gandhi and the Congress has been undertaken so far.

With the Hindus who have been blind devotees of Mr. Gandhi this study, although it is the first of its kind, will not find favour: indeed it is sure to provoke their wrath. How can it be otherwise when the conclusion arrived at is "Beware of Mr. Gandhi" ? Looking at it from a wider point of view, there is no reason for the Hindus to be enraged about it. The Untouchables are not the only community in India which thinks of Mr. Gandhi in these terms. The same view of Mr. Gandhi is entertained by the Muslims, the Sikhs and the Indian Christians. As a matter of fact, the Hindus should cogitate over the question and ask : why no community trusts Mr. Gandhi although he has been saying that he is the friend of the Muslims, Sikhs and the Scheduled Castes and what is the reason for this distrust ? In my judgment, there cannot be a greater tragedy for a leader to be distrusted by everybody as Mr. Gandhi is today. I am however certain that this is not how the Hindus will react. As usual, they will denounce the book and call me names. But as the proverb says: "The caravan must pass on, though the dogs bark." In the same way, I must do my duty, no matter what my adversaries may have to say. For as Voltaire observed: Who writes the history of his own time must expect to be attacked for everything he has said, and for everything he has not said: but these little drawbacks should not discourage a man who loves truth and liberty, expects nothing, fears nothing, asks nothing and limits his ambition to the cultivation of letters."

The book has become bulky. It may be said that it suffers by reason of over-elaboration and even by repetition. I am aware of this. But I have written the book especially for the Untouchables and for the foreigners. On behalf of neither could I presume knowledge of the relevant facts. For the particular audience I have in view, it is necessary for me to state both facts as well as arguments and pay no regard to the artistic sense or the fastidious taste of a cultivated and informed class of readers. As it is my intention to make the book a complete compendium of information regarding the movement of the Untouchables for political safeguards, I have added several appendices other than those of statistical character. They contain relevant documents both official and non-official which have a bearing upon the movement. Those who are interested in the problem of the Untouchables will, I believe, be glad to have this information ready at hand. The general reader may complain that the material in the Appendices is much too much. Here again, I must state that the Untouchables are not likely to get the information which to the general reader may be easily accessible. The test adopted is the need of the Untouchables and not of the general reader.

One last word. The reader will find that I have used quite promiscuously in the course of this book a variety of nomenclature such as Depressed Classes, Scheduled Castes, Harijans and Servile Classes to designate the Untouchables.

I am aware that this is likely to cause confusion especially for those who are not familiar with conditions in India. Nothing could have pleased me better than to have used one uniform nomenclature. The fault is not altogether mine. All these names have been used officially and unofficially at one time or other for the Untouchables. The term under the Government of India Act is 'Scheduled Castes.' But that came into use after 1935. Before that they were called 'Harijans" by Mr. Gandhi and 'Depressed Classes' by

Government. In a flowing situation like that it is not possible to fix upon one name, which may be correct designation at one stage and incorrect at another. The reader will overcome all difficulties if he will remember that these terms are synonyms and represent the same class. I am grateful to Professor Manohar Chitnis for the preparation of the Index and to Mr. S. C. Joshi for help in correcting the proofs.

B. R. AMBEDKAR.
22, Prithviraj Road,
New Delhi.
24th June 1945.

Thoughts on Linguistic States

Preface[xix]

The creation of Linguistic States is a burning question of the day. I regret that owing to my illness I was not able to take part in the debate that took place in Parliament much less in the campaign that is carried on in the country by partisans in favour of their views. The question is too important for me to sleep over in silence. Many have accused me for remaining quiet not knowing what the cause was.

I have therefore taken the other alternative i.e. to set out my views in writing.

Readers may find certain inconsistencies in my views as expressed in this brochure and as expressed formerly in certain public statements. Such changes in my view are, I am sure, very few. The former statements were made on the basis of fragmentary data. The whole picture was then not present to the mind. For the first time it met my eye when the report of the S.R.C. came out. This is sufficient justification for any change in my views which a critic may find.

To a critic who is a hostile and malicious person and who wants to make capital out of my inconsistencies my reply is straight. Emerson has said that consistency is the virtue of an ass and I don't wish to make an ass of myself. No thinking human being can be tied down to a view once expressed in the name of consistency. More important than consistency is responsibility. A responsible person must learn to unlearn what he has learned. A responsible person must have the courage to rethink and change his thoughts. Of course there must be good and sufficient reasons for unlearning what he has learned and for recasting his thoughts. There can be no finality in thinking.

The formation of Linguistic States, although essential, cannot be decided by any sort of hooliganism. Nor must it be solved in a manner that will serve party interest. It must be solved by cold blooded reasoning. This is what I have done and this is what I appeal to my readers to do.

B. R. AMBEDKAR

Milind Mahavidyalaya
Nagsen Vana, College Road
Aurangabad (Dn.)
23rd December 1955

India's Ancient Past Gave Place to Pessimism

'Rashtra Raksha Ke Vaidik Sadhan' by Swami Vedananda
Teertha

Preface[xx]

I am asked to write a Preface to the booklet by Swami Vedananda Teertha. Owing to pressure of work I had declined to accede to the request of the author. But as he has been insisting on my writing a few words, I have agreed to do so. The author's plea is that free India should adopt as its religion the gospel preached by the Vedas which is scattered all over the Vedas and which he has collected together in one place in this booklet. I do not know that the book will become the gospel of new India. But I can say that the book is not merely a wonderful collection of statements drawn from the Religious Books of the ancient Aryans but it brings out in a striking manner the vigour of thought and motion which prevailed among the ancient Aryans. What the book shows is that there is nothing in it of that pessimism among the ancient Aryans which dominates the modern Hindus. The work would have been of greater value if the author had considered why the positivism and optimism of India's ancient past gave place to the pessimism of later days. I hope that the author will deal with this problem at some later stage. In the meantime it is no small contribution to our knowledge that the theory that world is Maya is a new invention. It is from this point of view that I commend this booklet.

B. R. Ambedkar

PART 6 CONSTITUTIONAL WRITINGS

Dr Ambedkar had a clear understanding that constitutional methods would be the most effective way to bring about social and economic change compared to other measures. He was actively involved in drafting the constitution for India from 1924 onwards. His writings on Federation versus Freedom, his presentation to Simon Commission, and his memorandum prepared for the constituent assembly titled States and Minority were all exceptional. Dr Ambedkar faced numerous challenges while trying to get into the constituent assembly but he didn't give up. He wrote a memorandum to claim the rights of Scheduled Castes which proved fruitful later. He was not only inducted into the Constituent Assembly but also got an opportunity to head the drafting committee of the Constitution of India.

Dr Ambedkar's prefaces to some of his works dealing with the constitution process are included in this section, along with a foreword he wrote for a book by Divanji, which shared a Hindu Nationalist vision for the constitution. Although Dr Ambedkar was strongly opposed to this ideology, he accepted the offer to write the foreword but beautifully criticized the author's approach without compromising his own beliefs. Dr Ambedkar had a unique ability to use opportunities like these to counter opposing ideologies and promote truth. For instance, when he was asked to deliver a talk for Sai Devotees, he preached them the humanistic teachings of the Buddha and linked them with the humanitarian ideals of Sai Baba.

Lectures on the English Constitution

These are lectures on the English Constitution which I delivered to the students of the Government Law College, Bombay, in 1934-35. In publishing these lectures I have not forgotten how presumptuous it may be deemed for an Indian to attempt to expound the principles of the English Constitution. Sir Austen Chamberlain in the course of his cross-examination of a certain Indian witness who appeared before the Joint Committee on Indian Constitutional Reform observed: I listen to the witness with great respect when he talks of Indian conditions, but when he expounds the British Constitution he must permit me to remain of my own opinion (Minutes of Evidence, Vol. 11c, Q. 9812).

There is undoubtedly a great deal of truth in this remark and it should make every Indian who wishes to write on the English Constitution pause. An Indian, however, who wishes to enter into the field may well take courage from the fact that much of the English Constitution have been expounded by foreigners who have not only been heard with respect by Englishmen but whose writings have compelled a change of opinion. Be that as it may the remark made by Sir Austen Chamberlain need not come in my way. I am not expounding anything of my own. I am not expounding it to Englishmen. I am merely trying to make Dicey's English Constitution easier for Indian students to follow and to understand. From the stand-point of Indian students Dicey's treatise suffers from two defects.

It presupposes knowledge of certain parts of the English Constitution. For instance it presupposes knowledge of what is Parliament, how it is constituted and how it functions. This presupposition, howsoever justifiable it may be in the case of English students, would be without warrant in the case of Indian students who are called upon to take up the study of Dicey for the first time. Without a complete knowledge of this pan of the English Constitution Indian student feels completely bewildered and fails to grasp the full import of such fundamental principles as supremacy of the rule of law or the role of conventions in the working of the Constitution. In order that the Indian student may follow in an intelligent way the exposition of Dicey regarding the operation of these principles the teacher is forced at every turn to present to the student the framework of the English Constitution which finds no place in Dicey's treatise. Secondly, the English Constitution has grown enormously both as regards rules of law and also as regards conventions since the last edition of Dicey's English Constitution was published. The result of this growth has been felt in two different ways. It has rendered some of the illustrations given by Dicey quite inappropriate.

Secondly, it has altered the character of the English Constitution especially the relations of the Crown and the British Parliament to the Dominions to such an extent that an Indian student who depends upon Dicey alone will not be up-to-date but will be missing a great deal that is vital in it. Except for additions of matter and changes of form there is nothing new in these lectures. They constitute a revision of Dicey's treatise on the English Constitution with a view to remove its defects and to adapt it to the needs of Indian students.

A Report on the Constitution of the Government of Bombay Presidency

Preface[xxii]

I regret that I have not been able to agree in the tenor of the report prepared by my colleagues on the committee or to accept the more important of the conclusions on the matters falling within the scope of our inquiry. I have therefore submitted this separate report containing my own views and recommendations. The bulk of my report has exceeded that of my colleagues. It might perhaps have been possible, by including in my report nothing more than formal answers to the questions raised to limit its bulk. But I felt there was a question to which an answer could be given without some general explanation of the principles on which the answer was based or also the report could not be properly understood. I have therefore set aside all considerations of brevity which would have exposed me to the criticism that the recommendations in the report were not supported by a sufficient amount of reasons and arguments and have allowed the report to grow to the size it has reached.

States and Minorities

Preface[xxiii]

Soon after it became definite that the framing of the future Constitution of India was to be entrusted to a Constituent Assembly, the Working Committee of the All-India Scheduled Castes Federation asked me to prepare a Memorandum on the Safeguards for the Scheduled Castes for being submitted to the Constituent Assembly, on behalf of the Federation. I very gladly undertook the task. The results of my labour are contained in this brochure.

The Memorandum defines Fundamental Rights, Minority Rights and Safeguards for the Scheduled Castes. Those who hold the view that the Scheduled Castes are not a minority might say that in this matter I have gone beyond prescribed bounds. The view that the Scheduled Castes are not a minority is a new dispensation issued on behalf of the High and Mighty Hindu Majority which the Scheduled Castes are asked to submit to. The spokesmen of the Majority have not cared to define its scope and its meaning. Anyone with a fresh and free mind, reading it as a general proposition, would be justified in saying that it is capable of double interpretation. I interpret it to mean that the Scheduled Castes are more than a minority and that any protection given to the citizens and to the minorities will not be adequate for the Scheduled Castes. In other words it means that their social, economic and educational condition is so much worse than that of the citizens and other minorities that in addition to protection they would get as citizens and as minorities the Scheduled Castes would require special safeguards againstthe tyranny and discrimination of the majority.

The other interpretation is that the Scheduled Castes differ from a minority and therefore they are not entitled to the protection which can be claimed by a minority. This interpretation appears to be such unmitigated nonsense that no sane man need pay any attention to it. The Scheduled Castes must be excused if they ignore it. Those who accept my interpretation of the view that the Scheduled Castes are not a minority will, I am sure, agree with me that I am justified in demanding for the Scheduled Castes, all the benefit of the Fundamental Rights of citizens, all the benefit of the Provisions for the Protection of the minorities and in addition special Safeguards. The memorandum was intended to be submitted to the Constituent Assembly. There was no intention to issue it to the public. But my caste Hindu friends who have had the opportunity to read the typescript have pressed me to give it a wider circulation. Although it is meant for members of the Constituent Assembly, I do not see any breach of decorum in making it available to the general public. I have therefore agreed to fall in line with their wishes. Instead of setting out my ideas in general terms, I have drafted the Memorandum in the form of Articles of the Constitution. I am sure that for the sake of giving point and precision this method will be found to be more helpful. For the benefit of the Working Committee of the Scheduled Castes Federation, I had prepared certain explanatory notes and other statistical material. As the notes and the statistical material are likely to be useful to the general reader, I have thought it better to print them along with the Memorandum rather than keep them back. Among the many problems the Constituent Assembly has to face, there are two which are admittedly most difficult. One is the problem of the Minorities and the other is the problem of the Indian States.

I have been a student of the problem of the Indian States and I hold some very definite and distinct views on the subject. It was my hope that the Constituent Assembly would elect me to the States Committee Evidently, it has found men of superior calibre for the work. It may also be because I am one of those who are outside the tabernacle and therefore undesirable. I am not sorry to find myself left out. My only regret is that I have lost an opportunity to which I was looking forward for placing my views for the consideration of the Committee. I have therefore chosen to do the next best thing—namely, to incorporate them in this brochure along with the Rights of Citizens, of Minorities and of the Scheduled Castes so that a wider public may know what they are, may value them for what they are worth and may make such use of them as it may deem fit.

"Raja Graha"
B. R. AMBEDKAR
Dadar, Bombay
14 15-3-47

Indian Political Riddle

A book by Divanji

Foreword[xxiv]

Mr. Divanji is an old veteran savant and it is surprising to me that he should need someone like me to chaper on his debut in the world of political literature. But more surprising than this is that he should have fallen upon me as the 'person best fitted for this work. If at all he wanted anyone to do so, I think he should ·have approached the President of the Hindu Mahasabha; for much that forms the basis of Mr. Divanji's brochure, is a chip of the same block which forms the creed of the Hindu Mabasabha. Since Mr. Divanji insists on my writing a 'Foreword-.and that is I believe largely because I am now Executive Councillor I gladly do so, more especially on account of my association with him at Bombay Bar. There can be no exaggeration in saying that there is more talk of constitutional advancement in India, but very much less application to the problems involved in the making -of the Constitution itself. In view of the bewildering multiplicity of points of view and claims for protection, there can be no doubt that safety lies in having a multiplicity of plans designed from different angles for framing the constitution. As a new approach to the problem, this brochure will no doubt be welcomed by the public. But there is also another reason for welcoming this addition to the political literature of the country. Mr. Divanji makes an original approach for solving what he describes as the Indian political riddle. We have altogether three approaches, for the solution of this riddle-the purely territorial, the purely communal and the purely occupational. To these Mr Divanji adds the cultural approach.

I do not know how far his approach will find ready acceptance from those whose task it will be to frame the new Constitution. I have my own doubts about this plan. Some of his concrete proposals would be regarded as retrograde by the advanced politicians whose one -conserving passion is to achieve complete independence for India. For myself the cultural approach, so far as the Hindu group is concerned, may have a very deleterious effect upon the sub-merged sections of the Hindu population. Mr. Divanji in his booklet refers to the wars between the Brahmans and the Kshatriyas in ancient times wars in which each class vowed to exterminate the other. Mr. Divanji also brings out the fact that the two classes after a long and bloody struggle arrived at a compromise. This is good and sound history. But when Mr. Divanji further proceeds to state that compromise had established such harmonious relations between not only the two rival communities but also between them and the Banias (the Vaisyas) and the Sudras that never again in the long history of the Indian civilisation was there a recurrence of the internecine wars of the Vedic age above referred to, one is compelled to ask; 'Yes, peace! but peace of what kind? Was it peace with honor for the Vaisyas; and the Sudras or was it peace brought about by the suppression of the Vaisyas and the Sudras by a conspiracy between the Brahmanas and the Kshatriyas who compromised their quarrels so as not to weaken their ranks and with a. combined force to be better able to put down the rising tide, of the Vaisyas and Sudras which was taking place under thereligion of Buddha? This attitude is typical of the high-class Hindus. It givesthe clue to a proper understanding of how the higher class Hindus coming from the Brahmanas and Kshatriyas have developed an attitude of indifference towards the Vaisyas. and the Sudras have developed a self-satisfying frame of mind that there is nothing wrong with the Hindu society or with any of the numerous sections of which it is' composed. In coming to these conclusions, Mr. Divanji is unconsciously exhibiting the attitude of the higher classes towards the lower classes in Hindu society. It is this attitude which one finds ingrained in the congress policy which holds to the' view that for political purposes no distinction ought to be made between the high and the low and that all power may' be allowed to pass into the hands of those who are higher up in Hindu society and that no means need necessarily be adopted to empower those who are lower, to protect themselves against the injustices of the higher. That has been the tragedy of Hindu India, and I have no doubt that it will be so in the future under Swaraj unless proper precautions are taken to guard against the result. Mr. Divanji"s cultural approach will no doubt be examined by those who have a doubt whether it would be safe to leave the destinies of the suppressed and the oppressed in the bands of those who for centuries past have been responsible for reducing them to that status.

B. R. AMBEDKAR
New Delhi,
20th August, 1942.

PART 7 ECONOMICS

Dr. Ambedkar was truly a master of many subjects, as evidenced by the wide range of research topics he pursued throughout his career. However, he was particularly skilled in the area of economics, or political economy, which was his main focus of study. In fact, he earned his doctorate in this field, and his writing style was just as revolutionary and straightforward as in his other areas of expertise. Despite facing objections from his PhD guide, who wanted him to tone down his writing style, Dr. Ambedkar remained true to his vision and ultimately succeeded in making a significant impact in the field. One of his most notable contributions was his research on the Problem of the Rupee, which helped to establish the Reserve Bank of India (RBI).

Evolution of Provincial Finance in British India

Preface[xxv]

For a long time to come students will be saved the conventional humiliation of making an apology for presenting a study of Indian Finance or Economics. But it will, on the other hand, be necessary, I fear, for an equally long period, for them to tender an apology for the shortcomings of their respective investigations. Even when the treatment of a subject is analytical, a good analytical study often requires an historical setting. Unfortunately no spade-work has been done in the field of Indian Finance. Consequently the difficulties which beset a pioneer in that field are immense.

There is occasionally the difficulty owing to the antecedents of some point not having been quite completely elucidated. Often there is the apprehension of some error having crept in, and, when there is hardly anyone to save the student from it, there is nothing but to smart under a sense of irritating affliction. Not very seldom does it happen that a pioneer student is jubilant over his find of material bearing on his subject, but it is not without a long and wearisome search that he is able to sift the grain from the chaff. Again, sources sometimes prove false guides, so that a perusal of them only ends in a considerable waste of time and energy. Precisely these have been the difficulties besetting the present task.

There are no books to prepare the student for his work and hardly any savant to lighten his labour or set him on the proper track. Notwithstanding such odds, an attempt is made to make this study thorough without being too detailed. This has rendered the undertaking quite a laborious one. But I do not wish to speak of the labour that is involved, nor do I wish to astonish the reader with what might appear to be a formidable list of books and documents consulted in the preparation of this monograph. What I am anxious to speak of are its shortcomings. There are indeed many of them which a well-versed critic may spot out. It is my hope that they are not of such a character as seriously to impair the value which this monograph may otherwise be said to possess. My regrets are with regard to only a few of them.

I have specified a date as to when Local Decentralization of Finance commenced in India; but I feel that that date may not be the earliest and that there may be a date earlier than that one given by me. I wish I had settled that point finally. But that would have been a task analogous to that of searching for a needle in a haystack, and it is doubtful whether the value of that result would have been commensurate with that labour. Besides, although I am not confident of my date, my feeling is that later researches may after all confirm my statement. Another matter which I have not dealt with, but which I would have liked to have dealt with, was the inter-relation of Provincial and Local Finance. This I had originally planned to do, but left pursuing it because I found that the chief subject I was dealing with, namely, the Provincial Decentralization of Imperial Finance, began to be overlaid by facts and arguments not germane to that topic.

These shortcomings will, however, be removed by a supplementary monograph on Local Finance in British India, which is well under way and which I hope to publish before long. Occasional repetitions may also be pointed out as a defect of this monograph. That they should be avoided is all very well. But where economy in the words of explanation are likely to obscure, repetitions such as are unavoidable must be justified, for the interests of clarification should always outweigh the tedium they involve. I cannot conclude this preface without thanking Mr. Robinson, the Financial Secretary at the India Office, for many valuable suggestions and for the loan of many important documents bearing on the subject. I am also thankful to Prof. Cannan, of the University of London, who has read the rough draft of a small part of the manuscript. My debt to Prof. Seligman, my teacher at Columbia University, is of course immense : for from him I learned my first lessons in the theory of Public Finance. I am obliged to my friend Mr. C. S. Deole for assistance afforded in the dreary task of reading the proofs.

Foreword by Prof. Seligmen

The problem discussed by Mr. Ambedkar in his excellent dissertation is one that is arousing a growing interest in all parts of the world. From the very beginning we find fiscal burdens imposed by both central and local governments. As soon as there was a political organization, the conduct of war on the one hand and the provision of local protection and convenience on the other called for expenditures on the part of both state and local authorities. It was only at a later period that there was interpolated between the local and the central political organizations the intermediate form which Mr. Ambedkar calls the provincial government. The names applied to these various classes of expenditure differ with the authorities themselves. In India we speak of local, provincial, and imperial expenditure; in Germany, of local, state, and imperial expenditure; in the United States and Switzerland, of local, state, and federal expenditure; in Australia, of local, state, and commonwealth expenditure; in South Africa and Canada, of local, provincial, and federal expenditure; and in France, of local, departmental, and general expenditure.

In some cases, as in the British Empire, there is being developed a still more comprehensive class of expenditures, borne by the empire at large. The character and importance of these various classes of expenditure and the relations between them are undergoing a continual change, due to an alteration in the functions of government. This is itself largely due to a change in the general economic conditions, resulting in a gradual modification either of political structure or of administrative activity. In some countries, as in Canada, Argentine and Brazil, the provinces are really a creation of the central government; in other countries, as in the United States, Germany, and Switzerland, the federal government is the creation of the originally sovereign states. In some countries the intermediate (provincial or state) government is suffering a loss of importance as compared with the local or central governments; in other countries, the reverse is true. With the increasing pressure of taxation and the development under modern democracies of augmented governmental functions, the problem of the equitable distribution of burden among these various forms of government is becoming more or less acute. What Mr. Ambedkar calls assignments, assigned revenue, and share revenue, is symptomatic of the choice of methods in all countries.

One of three fundamental plans must be pursued. Either the central or the provincial government may be maintained by the other, according to the relative degree of strength : in former times, in the United States, and in Germany the states were supposed to support the central government, either wholly or in large measure; in modern times, in Canada and Australia, the reverse is true. Or, secondly, distinct revenues may be allocated to the separate governments : until recently the federal government in the United States, Germany, and Switzerland was supported primarily by indirect taxes; the state governments by direct taxes. Or, thirdly, the revenues may be collected by one government and a portion of the proceeds allotted to the other : there are many instances of a state or provincial tax being shared with the federal government, and still more examples of a federal or central tax being shared with the state or provincial government. In the United States at present the proper disposition of the inheritance tax as between state and federal government is fast becoming a burning question; in Germany the fiscal relations of state and federal government are in the forefront of political discussion.

The value of Mr. Ambedkar's contribution to this discussion lies in the objective recitation of the facts and the impartial analysis of the interesting development that has taken place in his native country. The lessons are applicable to other countries as well; nowhere, to my knowledge, has such a detailed study of the underlying principles been made. It is true that only half of the picture is presented. For the situation has everywhere been complicated by the entrance of the local authorities into the field; and by their claims to fiscal consideration as compared with both state (provincial) and general (federal) demands. In the United States, for instance, the now widely debated problem of financing the schools is largely dependent for its solution on the proper answer to be given to the question of fiscal interrelations. To this question Mr. Ambedkar proposes to devote himself in a subsequent study. If he succeeds in illumining that situation as successfully as he here deals with the initial problem, he will lay us all under still deeper obligations.

EDWIN R. A. SELIGMAN
COLUMBIA UNIVERSITY, NEW YORK,
October, 1924

The Problem of the Rupee

Preface to the First Edition

In the following pages I have attempted an exposition of the events leading to the establishment of the exchange standard and an examination of its theoretical basis.

In endeavouring to treat the historical side of the matter, I have carefully avoided repeating what has already been said by others. For instance, in treating of the actual working of the exchange standard, I have contented myself with a general treatment just sufficiently detailed to enable the reader to follow the criticism I have offered. If more details are desired they are given in all their amplitude in other treatises. To have reproduced them would have been a work of supererogation ; besides it would have only obscured the general trend of my argument. But in other respects, I have been obliged to take a wider historical sweep than has been done by other writers. The existing treatises on Indian currency do not give any idea, at least an adequate idea, of the circumstances which led to the reforms of 1893. I think that a treatment of the early history is quite essential to furnish the reader with a perspective in order to enable him to judge for himself the issues involved in the currency crisis and also of the solutions offered. In view of this, I have gone into that most neglected period of Indian currency extending from 1800 to 1893. Not only have other writers begun abruptly the story of the exchange standard, but they have popularized the notion that the exchange standard is the standard originally contemplated by the Government of India. I find that this is a gross error. Indeed, the most interesting point about Indian currency is the way in which the gold standard came to be transformed into a gold exchange standard. Some old, but by now forgotten, facts had therefore, to be recounted to expose this error.

On the theoretical side, there is no book but that of Professor Keynes which makes any attempt to examine its scientific basis. But the conclusions he has arrived at are in sharp conflict with those of mine. Our differences extended to almost every proposition he has advanced in favour of the exchange standard. This difference proceeds from the fundamental fact, which seems to be quite overlooked by Professor Keynes, that nothing will stabilize the rupee unless we stabilize its general purchasing power. That the exchange standard does not do. That standard concerns itself only with symptoms and does not go to the disease: indeed, on my showing, if anything, it aggravates the disease.

When I come to the remedy, I again find myself in conflict with the majority of those who like myself are opposed to the exchange standard. It is said that the best way to stabilize the rupee is to provide for effective convertibility into gold. I do not deny that this is one way of doing it. But, I think, a far better way would be to have an inconvertible rupee with a fixed limit of issue. Indeed, if I had any say in the matter, I would propose that the Government of India should melt the rupees, sell them as bullion and use the proceeds for revenue purposes and fill the void by an inconvertible paper. But that may be too radical a proposal, and I do not therefore press for it, although I regard it as essentially sound. In any case, the vital point is to close the Mints, not merely to the public, as they have been, but to the Government as well. Once that is done, I venture to say that the Indian currency, based on gold as legal tender with a rupee currency fixed in issue, will conform to the principles embodied in the English currency system.

It will be noticed that I do not propose to go back to the recommendations of the Fowler Committee. All those, who have regretted the transformation of the Indian currency from a gold standard to a gold exchange standard, have held that everything would have been all right if the Government had carried out in to the recommendations of that Committee. I do not share that view. On the other hand, I find that the Indian currency underwent that transformation because the Government carried out those recommendations. While some people regard that Report as classical for its wisdom, I regard it as classical for its nonsense. For I find that it was this Committee which, while recommending a gold standard, also recommended and thereby perpetuated the folly of the Herschell Committee, that Government should coin rupees on its own account according to that most naive of currency principles, the requirements of the public, without realizing that the latter recommendation was destructive of the former. Indeed, as I argue, the principles of the Fowler Committee must be given up, if we are to place the Indian currency on a stable basis.

I am conscious of the somewhat lengthy discussions on currency principles into which I have entered in treating the subject. My justification of this procedure is two-fold. First of all, as I have differed so widely from other writers on Indian currency, I have deemed it necessary to substantiate my viewpoint, even at the cost of being charged with over-elaboration. But it is my second justification, which affords me a greater excuse. It consists in the fact that I have written primarily for the benefit of the Indian public, and as their grasp of currency principles does not seem to be as good as one would wish it to be, an over-statement, it will be agreed, is better than an understatement of the argument on which I have based my conclusions.

Up to 1913, the Gold Exchange Standard was not the avowed goal of the Government of India in the matter of Indian Currency, and although the Chamberlain Commission appointed in that year had reported in favour of its continuance, the Government of India had promised not to carry its recommendations into practice till the war was over and an opportunity had been given to the public to criticize them. When, however, the Exchange Standard was shaken to its foundations during the late war, the Government of India went back on its word and restricted, notwithstanding repeated protests, the terms of reference to the Smith Committee to recommending such measures as were calculated to ensure the stability of the Exchange Standard, as though that standard had been accepted as the last word in the matter of Indian Currency. Now that the measures of the Smith Committee have not ensured the stability of the Exchange Standard, it is given to understand that the Government, as well as the public, desires to place the Indian Currency System on a sounder footing. My object in publishing this study at this juncture is to suggest a basis for the consummation of this purpose.

I cannot conclude this preface without acknowledging my deep sense of gratitude to my teacher, Prof. Edwin Cannan, of the University of London (School of Economics). His sympathy towards me and his keen interest in my undertaking have placed me under obligations which I can never repay. I feel happy to be able to say that this work has undergone close supervision at his hands, and although he is in no way responsible for the views I have expressed. I can say that his severe examination of my theoretic discussions has saved me from many an error. To Professor Wadia, of Wilson College, I am thankful for cheerfully undertaking the dry task of correcting the proofs.

Preface to the Second Impression

THE PROBLEM OF THE RUPEE was first published in 1923. Ever since its publication it has had a great demand : so great that within a year or two the book went out of print. The demand for the book has continued, but unfortunately I could not bring out a second edition of the book for the reason that my changeover from economics to law and politics left me no time to undertake such a task. I have, therefore, devised another plan : it is to bring out an up-to-date edition of the History of Indian Currency and Banking in two volumes, of which The Problem of the Rupee forms volume one. Volume two will contain the History of Indian Currency and Banking from 1923 onwards. What is therefore issued to the public now is a mere reprint of The Problem of the Rupee under a different name. I am glad to say that some of my friends who are engaged in the field of teaching economics have assured me that nothing has been said or written since 1923 in the field of Indian Currency which calls for any alteration in the text of The Problem of the Rupee as it stood in 1923. I hope this reprint will satisfy the public partially if not wholly. I can give them an assurance that they will not have to wait long for volume two. I am determined to bring it out with the least possible delay.

BR Ambedkar
Rajagraha,
Bombay,
7-5-1947.

Foreword by Professor Edwin Cannan

I am glad that Mr. Ambedkar has given me the opportunity of saying a few words about his book.

As he is aware, I disagree with a good deal of his criticism. In 1893, I was one of the few economists, who believed that the rupee could be kept at a fixed ratio with gold by the method then proposed, and I did not fall away from the faith when some years elapsed without the desired fruit appearing (see Economic Review, July 1898, pp. 400—403). I do not share Mr. Ambedkar's hostility to the system, nor accept most of his arguments against it and its advocates. But he hits some nails very squarely on the head, and even when I have thought him quite wrong, I have found a stimulating freshness in his views and reasons. An old teacher like myself learns to tolerate the vagaries of originality, even when they resist "severe examination" such as that of which Mr. Ambedkar speaks.

In his practical conclusion, I am inclined to think, he is right. The single advantage, offered to a country by the adoption of the gold-exchange system instead of the simple gold standard, is that it is cheaper, in the sense of requiring a little less value in the shape of metallic currency than the gold standard. But all that can be saved in this way is a trifling amount, almost infinitesimal, beside the advantage of having a currency more difficult for administrators and legislators to tamper with. The recent experience both of belligerents and neutrals certainly shows that the simple gold standard, as we understood it before the war, is not fool-proof, but it is far nearer being fool-proof and knave-proof than the gold-exchange standard. The percentage of administrators and legislators who understand the gold standard is painfully small, but it is and is likely to remain ten or twenty times as great as the percentage which understands the gold-exchange system. The possibility of a gold-exchange system being perverted to suit some corrupt purpose is very considerably greater than the possibility of the simple gold standard being so perverted.

The plan for the adoption of which Mr. Ambedkar pleads, namely that all further enlargement of the rupee issue should be permanently prohibited, and that the mints should be open at a fixed price to importers or other sellers of gold, so that in course of time India would have, in addition to the fixed stock of rupees, a currency of meltable and exportable gold coins, follows European precedents. In eighteenth-century England the gold standard introduced itself because the legislature allowed the ratio to remain unfavourable to the coinage of silver: in nineteenth-century France and other countries it came in because the legislatures definitely closed the mints to silver, when the ratio was favourable to the coinage of silver. The continuance of a mass of full legal tender silver coins beside the gold would be nothing novel in principle, as the same thing, though on a somewhat smaller scale, took place in France, Germany, and the United States.

It is alleged sometimes that India does not want gold coins. I feel considerable difficulty in believing that gold coins of suitable size would not be convenient in a country with the climate and other circumstances of India. The allegation is suspiciously like the old allegation that the " Englishman prefers gold coins to paper," which had no other foundation than the fact that the law prohibited the issue of notes for less than £ 5 in England and Wales, while in Scotland, Ireland, and almost all other English-speaking countries, notes for £ 1 or less were allowed and circulated freely. It seems much more likely that silver owes its position in India to the decision, which the Company made before the system of standard gold and token silver was accidentally evolved in 1816 in England, and long before it was understood, and that the position has been maintained, not because Indians dislike gold, but because Europeans like it so well that they cannot bear to part with any of it.

This reluctance to allow gold to go to the East is not only despicable from an ethical point of view. It is also contrary to the economic interest not only of the world at large, but even of the countries, which had a gold standard before the war and have it still or expect soon to restore it. In the immediate future, gold is not a commodity, the use of which it is desirable for these countries either to restrict or to economize. From the closing years of last century it has been produced in quantities much too large to enable it to retain its purchasing power and thus be a stable standard of value, unless it can constantly be finding existing holders willing to hold larger stocks, or fresh holders to hold new stocks of it. Before the war, the accumulation of hoards by various central banks in Europe took off a large part of the new supplies and prevented the actual rise of general prices being anything like what it would otherwise have been, though it was serious enough. Since the war, the Federal Reserve Board, supported by all Americans who do not wish to see a rise of prices, has taken on the new "White Man's Burden" of absorbing the products of the gold mines, but just as the United States failed to keep up the value of silver by purchasing it, so she will eventually fail to keep up the value of gold. In spite of the opinion of some high authorities, it is not at all likely that a renewed demand for gold reserves by the central banks of Europe will come to her assistance. Experience must gradually be teaching even the densest of financiers that the value of paper currencies is not kept up by stories of "cover" or "backing" locked up in cellars, but by due limitation of the supply of the paper. With proper limitation, enforced by absolute convertibility into gold coin which may be freely melted or exported, it has been proved by theory and experience that small holdings of gold are perfectly sufficient to meet all internal and international demands. There is really more chance of a great demand from individuals than from the banks. It is conceivable that the people of some of the countries, which have reduced their paper currency to a laughing stock, may refuse all paper and insist on having gold coins. But it seems more probable that they will be pleased enough to get better paper than they have recently been accustomed to, and will not ask for hard coin with sufficient insistence to get it. On the whole, it seems fairly certain that the demand of Europe and European-colonized lands for gold will be less rather than greater than before the war, and that it will increase very slowly or not at all.

Thus, on the whole, there is reason to fear a fall in the value of gold and a rise of general prices rather than the contrary.

One obvious remedy would be to restrict the production of gold by international agreement, thus conserving the world's resources in mineral for future generations. Another is to set up an international commission to issue an international paper currency so regulated in amount as to preserve an approximately stable value. Excellent suggestions for the professor's classroom, but not, at present at any rate nor probably for some considerable period of time, practical politics.

A much more practical way out of the difficulty is to be found in the introduction of gold currency into the East. If the East will take a large part of the production of gold in the coming years, it will tide us over the period which must elapse before the most prolific of the existing sources are worked out. After that we may be able to carry on without change or we may have reached the possibility of some better arrangement.

This argument will not appeal to those who can think of nothing but the extra profits which can be acquired during a rise of prices, but I hope it will to those who have some feeling for the great majority of the population, who suffer from these extra and wholly unearned profits being extracted from them. Stability is best in the long run for the community.

EDWIN CANNAN

The Commodity Exchanges in India

I am glad to respond to the request of Mr. SALVI to write a few words by way of introduction to his book on the Commodity Exchanges in India. It is obvious that his work if it is not a pioneering work is a more exhaustive piece of work than any that has so far appeared in the field. In nine chapters, he has examined the commodity exchanges in all their aspects and has thrown great light on an obscure subject. The subject of commodity exchanges is closely related to agriculture. India is an agricultural country and yet very little attention is paid to that subject. Those who are interested in the betterment of the agriculturists of India cannot but welcome the appearance of this comprehensive and instructive study.

BR Ambedkar
Bombay
29th December

Social Insurance and India

Foreword[xxvii]

Mr. M. R. IDGUNJI's book on Social Insurance and India is a well planned treatise.

It is divided into two parts. Part-I is general and deals with two main topics (I) the two principal branches of social insurance, viz., (i) Workmen's Compensation (ii) the different Financial aspects of Social insurance such as the Financial resources, the actuarial technique and financial administration. The discussion of the financial aspects of social insurance is aimed to explain the various problems connected with the financial resources required for the working of social insurance schemes, the various systems according to which the resources can be organised so as to have social insurance schemes working on sound lines and the problems of Administration connected with the financial side of social insurance.

Part-II deals with the problem of social insurance in relation to conditions prevalent in India. In this part the provision of the Indian Workmen's Compensation Act 1923, and of sickness Insurance are subjected to critical examination. In addition to this, there is a discussion of the Beveridge plan of Social Security and of the scheme of social security adopted in New Zealand. The discussion ends by an exploration of the possibilities for social security measures in India. The author holds the view that sound social insurance measures are not feasible in India unless certain fundamental difficulties are removed, and the country makes a substantial advance economically and is rid of the stark poverty that prevails in it today. The reasons in support of the stand he has taken are set out clearly and fearlessly. Realizing that India is predominantly an agriculture country and that the agriculture population sadly needs protection, the author has suggested a scheme of crop insurance based on the principles of social insurance. If indeed a scheme of crop insurance be evolved on the lines suggested by the author, it should go a long way in bettering the conditions of the rural masses in our country and lessening the terrors of famines.

Social insurance is a new thing in India. The Indian contribution to the literature on the subject is naturally meagre. In the circumstances, Mr. Idgunji's book is sure to be welcomed by all students of the subject both as an addition to the scanty literature thereon and also as a critical examination of the problems arising out of it. His style is lucid and his exposition is very clear.

B. R. AMBEDKAR

Notes and References

[i] BAWS Vol. 12

[ii] This text is provided by Eleanor Zelliot to Vasant Moon. Date mentioned April 6, 1956. Courtesy: 00_pref_unpub (franpritchett.com)

[iii] BAWS Vol. 11

[iv] BAWS Vol 17 Part 2, p. 86-87

[v] BAWS Vol. 4

[vi] What Follows is from Damet Ch.3 (old Testament)

[vii] BAWS Vol. 1

[viii] BAWS Vol 7

[ix] BAWS Vol 7

[x] Literature and life: A selection from the writings of Maxim Gorky.

[xi] Maxims and Reflections of Goethe, Nos. 453, 543.

[xii] This text is not actually a preface or introduction of Dr Ambedkar's unpublished book "Essays on Untouchables and Untouchability' but this portion is presented as chapter 1 under title 'Untouchability: Its Source ' in BAWS Vol 5. However, the presentation and style of this is in pattern of Ambedkar style of preface writing therefore to present the gist of this book, I have included this chapter here.

[xiii] BAWS Vol. 17 part 2, p. 64

[xiv] BAWS Vol 1

[xv] BAWS Vol 1

[xvi] BAWS Vol 8

[xvii] The Crisis of the National State (1943), p. 4.

[xviii] BAWS Vol 9

[xix] BAWS Vol 1

[xx] BAWS Vol 17 part 2, p 89 Swami Vedananda Teertha (1892-1956)—Rashtra Raksha Ke Vaidik Sadhan—1948

[xxi] BAWS Vol. 12 p. 155

[xxii] BAWS Vol. 2, p. 314

xxiii BAWS Vol 1, p. 381
xxiv Rare Prefaces by Bhagwan Das, pp.14-16
xxv BAWS Vol. 6
xxvi BAWS Vol 6, p. 692
xxvii BAWS Vol 6, p. 693-94